Up Against the Wal-Marts

SECOND EDITION

Up Against the WAL-MARTS

SECOND EDITION

*How Your Business Can Prosper in
the Shadow of the Retail Giants*

DON TAYLOR
and
JEANNE SMALLING ARCHER

AMACOM
American Management Association

New York • Atlanta • Brussels • Chicago • Mexico City • San Francisco
Shanghai • Tokyo • Toronto • Washington, D. C.

Special discounts on bulk quantities of AMACOM books are available to corporations, professional associations, and other organizations. For details, contact Special Sales Department, AMACOM, a division of American Management Association, 1601 Broadway, New York, NY 10019.
Tel.: 212-903-8316. Fax: 212-903-8083.
Web site: www.amacombooks.org

This publication is designed to provide accurate and authoritative information in regard to the subject matter covered. It is sold with the understanding that the publisher is not engaged in rendering legal, accounting, or other professional service. If legal advice or other expert assistance is required, the services of a competent professional person should be sought.

Taylor, Don (Donald D.)
    Up against the Wal-Marts : how your business can prosper in the shadow of the retail giants / Don Taylor, Jeanne Smalling Archer.— 2nd ed.
        p.   cm.
    Includes bibliographical references and index.
    ISBN 0-8144-7300-8
    1. Success in business.   2. Retail trade—Management.   3. Service industries—Management.   4. Small business—Management.   I. Archer, Jeanne Smalling.   II. Title.

HF5386.T319   2005
658.8'7—dc22

                                                                2005006314

Printing number

10   9   8   7   6   5   4   3   2   1

Contents

Acknowledgments

We owe a great debt of gratitude to all of you who directly or indirectly made this book possible. We appreciate and admire all of you entrepreneurs who have shared your stories, strategies, and successes. May you continue to prosper.

We are grateful to our friends at AMACOM who believed it was time for a new book and supported the work. We offer our special appreciation to friend and mentor Dr. Winston D. Stahlecker who made many excellent suggestions for improving the content.

Heartfelt thanks to the staff of the Harrington Cancer Center who are guiding coauthor Don Taylor through the maze of stem cell transplantation and related cancer treatments. And, finally thank you Sue and Christi for your love, support, and hard work.

Preface

"Wal-Mart put me out of business!" He almost shouted at us. We were waiting to tape the Phil Donahue show in New York City, and this Wal-Mart–bashing, failed small-business owner expected us to join him in blaming Wal-Mart for his failure.

However, we did not agree. Wal-Mart didn't put him out of business, nor have they put any other small-business owner out of business. That's not the way the game of business works. No big-box ever forced a single independent out of business. What these business giants do is give the customer a choice. It is always the customer who chooses which merchants go, and which remain. Your customers won't put you out of business as long as you are their best business choice.

The foundation of free enterprise is choice. You can choose to compete, you can choose to take on the giants, and you can choose to win. It isn't easy—nothing worthwhile ever is—but millions of small-business owners are prospering, and you can too. The only way to thrive in the changing game of business is to do the right things, and do them well.

If you're struggling as a business owner, this book can be your guide. If you're finding it harder to compete, we want to be your coach. If you want to be a winner, we can show you how. But there are three things you'll have to do.

1. You must be willing to make changes in your business. You'll need new strategies to take on your ever-advancing competitors.

2. You must use this book as your business study guide. Before you can do the right things, you have to know what they are. We've included the new best practices of small-business owners.

3. You must determine where you are and where you want to go. This book will help you lay out the steps to move your business to a position of strength, and it will show you how to be the best choice for more customers.

If you are willing to make changes, read on. Join us on a success journey as we track the fortunes of survivors who have gone up against the giants and won. We'll give you hundreds of examples of how independents, just like you, have learned to compete.

More importantly, you can learn how to grow and prosper in the changing business game, by learning from others' mistakes, and following their plans for success. We'll give you the strategies and tactics, but you must supply the will to win. It has been ten years since Jeanne Archer and I coauthored the original *Up Against the Wal-Marts*. Our goal was to write a best-seller that would help small-business owners compete with the power retailers of the day. Though we succeeded, and it is rewarding to know that the content of the original book has helped hundreds of thousands of small-business owners become more successful, there are still more challenges today.

Many things have changed in the business arena during the past ten years. New low-price leaders are emerging. Dollar General and Family Dollar chains are each *opening an average of two new stores every day*. These small-store chains target the lowest-income consumers, and promise low prices and quick shopping experiences in their mini (usually 8,000 to 10,000 square feet) stores.

Wal-Mart is still the largest retailer in the world. They lead number two Home Depot by more than $200 billion in sales.

Kmart, who was a strong retailer in 1994, has survived bankruptcy, and just completed a $12 billion merger with Sears. The new company, Sears Holdings Corp., is now the third-largest retailer.

Category killers are enjoying continuing success as they add locations and change their marketing mix. Walgreen Drugs racked up sales of $37.5 billion in FY 2004. Lowe's home improvement stores saw revenues top out at $36.5 billion last year. Office supply retailers, Staples and Office Depot, both topped $13 billion in sales. The big-boxes are still growing and changing.

The good news for those of you who are reading this book is that the best practices of successful small competitors are changing too. We are pleased to report that more than 90 percent of all the successful entrepreneurs we wrote about or profiled in the original *Up Against the Wal-Marts* are still in business today. Two owners retired with success, one business failed in 1995, and two other businesses have eluded our attempts to locate them. We assume they failed.

Those who are still with us are more than survivors; they are successes. But they too have made changes. In order to grow and expand, they have modified their best practices and refocused their operations. Some have taken on new lines. Others have repositioned to serve new customers. And some opened altogether new operations. The key is that they continue to change.

We've added to our historical perspective by working with thousands of additional small-business owners since 1994. We've learned from them all. As we share the *new best practices,* you will see that the new business owners and managers whose experience we share are just ordinary people like you. But the success they have achieved borders on extraordinary. These successful men and women have proven the premise of the original *Up Against the Wal-Marts*: Success in business is achieved by the doing the right things well. This new edition will give you the best practices of highly successful small-business owners.

We have included fourteen success strategies that independents are using to take on the mega-merchants. We have expanded the marketing mix, and included a new "four-fundamentals" approach for evaluating and improving your customer service.

You will find new tools for hiring first-rate employees. We have included dozens of tips on how to sell to differing groups of consumers. We have added nearly fifty low-cost promotion strategies, and included nearly 300 tips for improving nearly every aspect of your business.

We have devoted one entire chapter to providing you more than twenty new tools, including: The Thirty-Minute Checkup Tool, The Promotion Spending Guide, The BackTrac Financial Troubleshooter Tool, and The Customer Batting Average tool.

We have also included more than a dozen success profiles from small-business owners and managers just like you. You will learn what they are doing to grow their businesses at double—or even triple—digit rates.

We have added an entire chapter on beating burnout. You can use the fifteen-step process to have more fun and get more done.

Finally, we have added a Key Points Checklist at the end of every chapter. You can quickly review the most important concepts covered in that chapter.

Study the new best practices, use those that fit your business type, and take your business to the next level. Then tell us what you did. Who knows, there may be yet another edition of this book in the future.

Don Taylor
d_staylor@sbcglobal.net

The Game Is Changing

Change is the law of life. And those who look only to the past or the present are certain to miss the future.
—JOHN F. KENNEDY

Shopping malls, discount stores, and strip centers are replacing downtowns, CDs have replaced records and tapes, and computers have made typewriters obsolete for most word processing tasks. Digital images are replacing photographs, cell phones have replaced two-way radios, and the Internet is outpacing newspapers, television, and radio as the source for news.

Change is constantly occurring in all areas of society and in all parts of the world. Nowhere is change more important than in business. S. Robson Walton, chairman of Wal-Mart Stores, Inc., and son of Wal-Mart's founder, Sam Walton, said, "I learned from my dad that change and experimentation are constants and important. You have to keep trying new things."

Consumers and competitors drive change in the business world. Consumers are constantly redefining customer service and value. Customer clusters, such as the Baby Boomers and Generation X shoppers, continue to be moving targets that drive marketers crazy. These two generations have tremendous buying power, but as spenders they are unpredictable and difficult to pattern.

New competitors are constantly entering the marketplace and eliminating any current sustainable advantages. Even well-established companies are repositioning to capture elusive points of market share.

Grocery stores now sell gas, and gas stations now offer grocery items. Banks now sell insurance, and insurance companies now offer banking services.

Technology is another driving force behind change. The Internet has opened the way for millions of new and expanded businesses. Virtual retailers abound. Service firms offer great variety online. And even small manufacturers market their creations via this medium. For all businesses, point-of-sale, inventory tracking, data base management, financial analysis, and record keeping have never been easier or cost less to implement.

Patrick Henry, American statesman and patriot, said, "I know no way of judging the future but by the past." So as we seek the future of business success, perhaps a review of past performers is in order. Every company can teach us something about business. Even the poorest performers can serve as bad examples.

The Early Powerhouses

The first half of the twentieth century saw the arrival and growth of large retail giants. Sears, Roebuck, & Co., J.C. Penney, and Montgomery Ward were the three most dominant chains. Sears was the early pacesetter and sales leader.

These chains possessed real retail clout and set the standard for other retailers. Interestingly, the big three seemed to coexist easily with the independent merchants. Even the five-and-dime stores like S. S. Kresge, Woolworth's, and Mattingly's blended into, but did not dominate, the Main Street mix.

A New Breed Emerges

Then, in the early 1960s, a new breed of retailers emerged, led by S. S. Kresge's Kmart, The Dayton Company, and Sam Walton's Wal-Mart. This new group of discount stores redefined value and variety with low prices and wide inventories.

Kmart and Target experienced aggressive early growth, fueled by the strength of their parent companies. Wal-Mart's early growth was relatively slow, as the company opened fewer than 500 stores from 1962 through 1982.

Surprisingly, there was limited head-to-head competition between these four fast-rising discounters before the early 1980s. Kmart and Target worked regional metro areas, and no one thought Sam Walton's billion-dollar, small-town-only chain was any threat to the huge retailers of the day. In the 1980s, Sears still dominated the retail landscape, while hard-charging Kmart was just beginning to close the gap.

Other mega-competitors joined the fray in the 1970s and 1980s. The category killers entered solid retail markets like hardware, electronics, toys, and drugs, and attempted to strip out the entire trade segment. Early successes in this area were Walgreens drugstores, Toys "R" Us, and Home Depot. These three category specialists now have combined annual sales of more than $120 billion.

The wholesale club concept began in 1976 when Sol Price opened his first Price Club warehouse. From the beginning, these "members only" warehouses operated with the "stack it high and watch it fly" philosophy. There were no frills. Floors were concrete, shelves were metal, and overhead was low.

Survival of the Fittest

The easiest prey for the new breed of discount predators and category killers were the independent Main Street merchants who were still doing business as they had for years. They had invested little of their profits back into their businesses, and had grown complacent. Storefronts reflected this neglect with peeling paint, cracked windows, and general deterioration. Sidewalks cracked and buckled with minimal repair. Grass grew in the cracks, and litter lingered in the gutter.

Owners shortened business hours to accommodate their own lifestyles. Promotions were halfhearted, and few changes were made within stores. Layout, lighting, displays, and merchandising remained virtually unchanged. Only inventory changed, and often that was slow to follow newer trends and changing customer needs and desires.

Business was good enough to allow the relaxed owners to still earn a good living. However, many of these merchants had lost their first love—pleasing the customer.

Conditions Were Nearly Perfect

With an expanding highway system and more reliable transportation, customers were becoming more mobile. They were willing to drive fifty miles or more to shop. They were hungry for new experiences at a time when Main Street merchants were happy with the status quo. Conditions were nearly perfect for a shopping revolution.

The new breed of retailers led the revolution. They began to grab market share away from the established merchants with wide selections, low prices, and modern merchandising techniques. As business slowed on Main Street, many of the entrenched elite lamented their woes at the local coffee shop. Some went after legal solutions, claiming unfair pricing and competitive practices. Other sought political help with zoning and other "keep them away from our town" efforts. Most did nothing.

Small-business owners offered the new breed only moderate competition in most markets. Running profitable but inefficient businesses, the small retailers put little pressure on their suppliers to keep business costs low. Their "mark it up 40 percent across the board" philosophy left plenty of margin for the lean-operating discounters.

In addition, independent owners had no good source of information on how to combat the new breed. No book like the original *Up Against the Wal-Marts* existed. University professors, home economists, and consultants—none of whom had ever run a store or made a payroll—scurried around the country defining the problem, but offering only superficial solutions. Aggressive merchants were trying new things, but no one was sure what worked and what didn't.

Profiles of the New Breed

One of the success strategies detailed in Chapter Two is to study the success of others. The new breed brings strong challenges to you as an independent-business owner. To compete successfully, you must know the strengths and weaknesses of these companies. The more you know about your competitors, the better you are positioned to counter their strengths and capitalize on their weaknesses.

Wal-Mart, in a Class by Itself

Wal-Mart is still the largest retailer in the world. The number two retail competitor, Home Depot, has annual sales of about 25 percent of Wal-Mart's $285 billion. The number three retailer—the newly merged Kmart and Sears—has combined sales of $55 billion, or about 19 percent of Wal-Mart's total. Their nearest discount competitor, Target Corporation, has annual revenues of less than 16 percent of Wal-Mart's.

Not only is Wal-Mart big, but they are also respected in the business world. In February 2003, *Fortune* magazine published a survey of 10,000 business executives, directors, and security analysts. In the survey, Wal-Mart was named America's Most Admired Company.

Fifteen years ago, I doubt that you could have found any business analyst or futurist who would have predicted the Wal-Mart explosion of the 1990s. I'm certain no one on the fourteenth floor at General Motors believed they would be knocked out of the number one spot on the Fortune 500 list by a $20 billion small-town retailer from Arkansas. But that's exactly what happened in 2002.

After Sam Walton's death in 1992, the job of running Wal-Mart fell to the core group of high-level managers that Walton had assembled. They believed as he believed, and were nearly as committed to the Wal-Mart cause as Walton himself had been.

After grieving Walton's death, they went back to work. The result was an explosion of growth. Sales soared from $44 billion in FY 1992 to nearly $218 billion in FY 2002. Wal-Mart president and CEO H. Lee Scott casually mentioned this feat in his message to shareholders in the 2002 annual report. "Sales for the year ended January 31, 2002, were just under $218 billion, making us the largest company in the world as measured by annual revenue," he stated in the report. Scott went on to say that the company had never set a goal to become the biggest, but rather to be the best, retail company, as measured by customers, associates, suppliers, communities, and shareholders.

Wal-Mart was able to maintain double-digit sales growth for FY 2005. Annual revenues for the company came in at $285 billion, a real growth percentage of 11 percent over the previous year's sales. To put their size into perspective, it takes the sales of the next five largest retail competitors to equal one year of Wal-Mart's sales.

Wal-Mart is still primarily a North American company. Less than 20 percent of their revenues come from the International Division.

What's Next?

We predict that Wal-Mart will continue to grow. While the next ten years may not equal the explosive expansion of the past decade, look for continued growth in all divisions.

We believe the aggressive strategy of converting existing discount stores to Supercenters will continue. The Supercenters offer groceries, services, specialty lines, and a greatly expanded number of discount items. The larger Supercenters carry as many as 150,000 different inventory items (SKUs).

Another hot spot for growth is the Neighborhood Market concept. The number of these full-line grocery stores (supermarkets) grew at the rate of 63 percent in 2004, and we anticipate continued accelerated growth of this concept in the coming years.

When there is a Supercenter in every viable trade area and multiple stores in larger cities, we expect the company to use a "fill in" strategy. This may take the form of Wal-Mart Express stores or Neighborhood Markets. Kroger, Albertson's, Safeway, and some convenience store chains may feel added pressure in the grocery segment.

Given the success of Home Depot and Lowe's (more than $109 billion in combined revenues), we wouldn't be shocked to see an experimental Wal-Mart Home Center concept tried. Who wouldn't like to see a price rollback on 2-by-4s?

Nor would we be too surprised if a private-label auto retailing effort was launched. Imagine a Toyota Camry or a Ford Taurus with the Wal-Mart label, and service available 24/7 at your local Wal-Mart Supercenter.

Whatever Wal-Mart's actual marketing plans may be, one thing is certain: The company will continue to refine their competitive strategy, and keep pressure on all competitors large and small.

Other Big-Box Discounters

Target Corporation. Target is the second-largest discount retailer, based on annual revenue. Sales for FY2005 came in at $46.8 billion.

The chain has 1,308 stores, and began life as the discount arm of old-line retailer Dayton Company. Like Wal-Mart and Kmart, the first Target store opened in 1962.

Target recently became the tail that wagged the dog. On January 31, 2000, Dayton-Hudson Corporation (formerly the Dayton Company) changed their name officially to Target Corporation. This was done to reflect the fact that Target stores comprised more than 75 percent of the company's sales and profits.

Target Corporation also owns the Mervyn's and Marshall Field's chains. At this time, Target has proposed selling the two smaller chains in order to focus on the Target discount store concept.

Target's reputation as "the upscale discounter" seems to still be intact, and the stores remain focused on brand names, designer lines, bright lights, wide aisles, and low-hassle checkouts. However, the chain's strength of position may be eroding as Wal-Mart continues to open their newer, brighter, user-friendly Supercenters. The upscale image differences are disappearing.

Target Corporation currently operates fewer than one hundred SuperTargets, which include groceries, and are direct competition to Wal-Mart's Supercenters. Growth of the SuperTargets has been slow, and given Wal-Mart's grocery success, one might wonder if revenue generated from the sale of Marshall Field's and Mervyn's might not speed up the rollout of SuperTargets.

Although Target has moved into the "number two" discounter position, they were passed by hard-charging Home Depot in the annual sales race. Target ranks number four on *STORES Magazine's* Top 100 Retailers list behind Wal-Mart, Home Depot, and Kroger.

Kmart Corp. At age 40, Kmart experienced a midlife crisis. Plagued by slowing sales and bottom-line losses, the company filed for Chapter 11 bankruptcy protection on January 22, 2002.

A new company, Kmart Holding Corporation, emerged from the bankruptcy proceedings in May 2003, with a court-approved plan for reorganization. Under the leadership of 42-year-old billionaire Edward S. Lampert, the resurrected Kmart produced four straight quarters of profitability. In early 2005, Lampert, who owned a 15 percent stake in Sears, Roebuck and Company, merged the two retail giants into one company known now as Sears Holdings Corporation. Combined, the two firms generate $55 billion in revenue, making the new company the third-largest retailer in America.

Industry analysts expect the company to convert about 400 of Kmart's premium locations to upscale Sears stores. It is likely that low-performing Kmart stores will be closed to bolster profits and keep stock prices up.

Lampert has a reputation for penny pinching and tight cost control reminiscent of the late Sam Walton. Whether Lampert can match Walton's growth, customer satisfaction, and value delivery remains to be seen.

Small-Store Discounters

Though dollar stores have been around for nearly fifty years, it is only of late that their expansion has become noticeably aggressive. In some cases, these "mini-marts" have opened more than one hundred stores in a single month, and their numbers are skyrocketing. Dollar General and Family Dollar are the leaders. These chains are narrowly positioned to accommodate low-priced buyers and have two central promotion themes: Save time, and save money.

Dollar stores generally target the bottom layer of the socioeconomic strata. According to A.C. Nielsen's *Consumer Insight Magazine*, a typical shopper is "the female head of household, thirty-five to fifty-four years old, in the low- to middle-income bracket." The magazine goes on to define other typical customers as "retired shoppers on fixed incomes."

Dollar stores are usually small (6,000 to 10,000 square feet), do minimal advertising, and rely on their "low price" reputation to attract customers. They carry a relatively small number of SKUs, usually between 4,000 and 6,000 different items.

The success of these small-store discounters can be attributed to four main factors. First, they offer a strong value proposition tied to very low prices. This operational philosophy mimics Wal-Mart's early days. Second, they provide a small-store format that allows a "quick-in-and-out" shopping experience. Third, they focus on high-volume, fast-moving inventory. And fourth, they know their target customers well, and are aggressive in opening store locations that are convenient to their customer base.

Dollar General Corporation. The biggest kid on the dollar store block is Dollar General. They were ranked in the top 40 on The National Retail Federation's *STORES Magazine* Top 100 Retailers list with sales of $7.66 billion in FY 2005.

Founder J. C. Turner opened the first store in May of 1955 in Springfield, Kentucky. By 1965, the chain had opened 255 dollar stores. Dollar General's corporate offices are located in Goodlettsville, Tennessee.

The company added stores over the years by purchasing other small chains and opening stores sporadically. Fueled by strong financial success in the early 1990s, Dollar General began serious expansion in multiple markets. In February 2004, the company opened a record 119 stores in a single month. Dollar General now operates more than 7,000 stores in thirty states. Only seven of those states are west of the Mississippi River. Like the early days of Wal-Mart, most of Dollar General's stores are located in small to midsize markets. This will change in coming years, as the chain is now opening multiple stores in communities with populations of 100,000 or more.

Family Dollar Stores, Incorporated. The Family Dollar chain is one of the fastest-growing discount store chains in the United States. In the past five years, the company has averaged opening 400 new stores each year. They recently announced plans to open 565 new stores in FY 2004.

This chain, like Dollar General, targets low- to moderate-income customers. They tout low prices, offered in a no-frills, low overhead, self-service environment.

Family Dollar opened its seven-thousandth store in June of 2004. The company generated combined annual revenues of nearly $5.28 billion in FY 2004. Founded in 1959, the company headquarters are in Matthews, North Carolina, near Charlotte. The company operates stores in forty-three states.

Family Dollar is unique among a plethora of fast-growth competitors in that they have no long-term debt. Most of the stores are located in leased properties. Their concept is working, and we expect them to gain ground on Dollar General.

Category Killers

The term "category killers" is used to describe a powerful, fast-growing breed of specialty retail discounters. These "power nichers" are more narrowly focused than the big-box discounters. Generally, they target one industry segment and related lines.

They carry most of the national brands at low prices, and have fairly low levels of customer service. While there are companies who claim to offer higher levels of service, the typical category-killer customer doesn't expect to get a lot of help.

In this area of retail, there is currently more head-to-head competition than any other. The biggest of the great battles is currently being waged between number two retailer Home Depot and number twelve Lowe's. Although Home Depot is more than twice the size of Lowe's, Lowe's has aggressively waded into the Atlanta market (Home Depot's headquarters).

The second great battle has been going on since 1994 when the original *Up Against the Wal-Marts* book was written. This battle involves number fifteen retailer, Best Buy, and number thirty, Circuit City. In FY 1994, Circuit City recorded more than $4 billion in sales while Best Buy rang up only $3 billion. In the following decade, hard-charging Best Buy grew to nearly $21 billion while Circuit City languishes at about $10 billion. While the battle still rages, for the moment Best Buy has the upper hand.

Home Depot. Home Depot is the "King-Kong" of category killers. With annual sales of $73.1 billion, the Atlanta-based chain ranks as the second-largest retailer in America. In early 2005, the company operated a total of 1,895 stores throughout the United States, Canada, and Mexico.

Perhaps one of the most interesting aspects of Home Depot is that the company is one of the younger chains in retail. Founded in 1978, the company hit $50 billion in revenues in its twenty-third year. No one, including Wal-Mart, has achieved that kind of growth.

Home Depot stores average 107,000 square feet, and house 40,000 to 50,000 different inventory items. The typical store carries building materials, home improvement supplies, landscaping and garden products, tools, and appliances.

One of Home Depot's marketing strategies is to position each store as a "home improvement resource." A place where customers come in "wondering how," and leave "knowing how." Do-it-yourself classes are held in each store to teach basic skills such as plumbing, patio building, and electrical wiring. And, of course, attendees are more likely to leave armed with all the tools and materials to get the job done. Larger tools, such as concrete mixers, garden tillers, and masonry saws, can be rented at more than 600 Home Depot stores. This expands the capacity of the customer who wants to do his or her own work to save money.

Home Depot has also positioned itself as "the place" for small contractors, remodelers, and specialty trade professionals. They provide separate checkout and help areas, credit card programs, and delivery for this customer segment.

Lowe's. At $36.5 billion in annual revenues, Lowe's is the second-largest seller of home improvement products in America, and ranks as the number twelve retailer overall. Sales and profits from the company are at all-time highs, and even same-store sales increased by 7 percent last year.

In the battle with Home Depot, Lowe's is the hard-charging aggressor. In the past five years, they marched into Home Depot's headquarters city, Atlanta, much as General Sherman did 140 years ago. Many retail analysts believe that Home Depot is now on the defensive. For years they have been proactive in the marketplace. They now find themselves reacting to aggressive marketing efforts by Lowe's.

Lowe's is based in Wilkesboro, North Carolina, and has nearly 1,000 stores. Lowe's stores have a softer, more appealing look both inside and outside. While they are a big-box chain, their decor and merchandising is currently more upscale than Home Depot's.

Women seem more comfortable in the Lowe's atmosphere, and since women drive most of the home decorating projects and greatly influence home remodeling decisions, the softer appeal seems to be working.

Lowe's wins the battle for dollar generated per customer per store visit. The average Lowe's shopper drops $56.28 per visit, compared to Home Depot's average ticket of $51.29. However, Home Depot wins the sales per square foot award with $370 per square foot, compared to Lowe's $294.

Lowe's strongest area is the sale of appliances. The chain sells more than 14 percent of all appliances sold in the United States. Home Depot has only a 6.2 percent market share. Sears is the all-time appliance sales leader and still holds nearly 40 percent of total U.S. appliance sales. However, that share is eroding, and Lowe's and Home Depot are the wind and rain.

Walgreen Company. With $37.5 billion in revenues in FY 2004, Walgreens is the largest and fastest-growing drugstore chain in America. The company has expanded rapidly in the past decade and ranks as the number eleven retailer in the United States.

Since 1993, the company has opened 2,800 stores, and now operates more than 4,800 stores in 44 states and Puerto Rico. This is a fast-growing, aggressive company that plans to have 7,000 retail outlets opened by 2010.

Walgreens captured 13 percent of the entire U.S. prescription market in 2003 by filling more than 400 million prescriptions. The company estimates that 62 percent of the U.S. population lives within five miles of a Walgreens store.

Although its roots go back to 1901, Walgreens may be the "newest" drugstore chain in the industry. More than two-thirds of their stores are less than ten years old.

While many small, independent pharmacies are very vocal in their concerns about Wal-Mart, Walgreens may be a bigger threat. Their goal is to saturate markets so that no customer is more than two miles away from a Walgreens store.

Nearly 25 percent of Walgreens locations are open twenty-four hours, and their merchandising is excellent. This contributes to their ability to generate $677 per square foot in sales.

Another indication of how tough Walgreens is as a competitor can be seen in their definition of "customer service." President and COO Jeff Rein defines service differently than most independents. Rein describes service as "locations, hours, store layout, easy access, targeted merchandise selection, and fast service."

Rein's service definition can be translated into sales growth, strong earnings, and a strong balance sheet. It also appears to be a definition for continued success.

Best Buy Company, Inc. In 1994, we called Best Buy an up-and-comer in the consumer electronics, appliances, and home-office technology industry. Now they have firmly established themselves as the dominant industry leader, primarily through an aggressive acquisition strategy.

Sales for FY2004 hit an all-time high of $24.5 billion, a 17 percent increase over the previous year. More than 1,500 stores have been added to the chain in the past five years. The additions have come through building new stores and acquisitions of Future Shop (a Canadian retail chain of 95 stores), Magnolia Hi-Fi (13 stores), Media Play (76 stores), On Cue and Sam Goody, (850 stores), and Suncoast (400 stores).

Best Buy was one of the leanest firms in retail, and they consistently ran their stores on minimal operating expenses. In 1995 and 1996, the company reported selling, general, and administrative (SG&A) expenses as 11.2 percent and 11.3 percent, respectively. From 1997 through 2000, SG&A expenses were held under 15 percent of sales. However, with huge acquisitions often come inefficiencies. In FY 2002, SG&A expenses soared to 17.8 percent and then took a huge jump again in FY 2003 to 20.2 percent. FY 2004 saw a small dip, as operating expenses dropped to 19.9 percent of sales.

To overcome these higher operating expenses, Best Buy has raised their selling prices in relation to their purchasing cost. The result is a gross profit margin of 25.2 percent in FY 2004 compared to 12.9 percent in FY 1996. Translated to customer value, the customer is now getting less product for the dollars they spend at Best Buy.

Best Buy is targeting younger consumers. This is apparent in the nature of the stores they have acquired, the overall product mix, store atmosphere, and advertising. While their marketing strategy seems to be working for now, Best Buy may find that older consumers are seeking alternatives because of loud music, funky lighting, and youthful associates.

As we go to press, Best Buy has announced plans to sell off some of their recent acquisitions. Perhaps, like Kmart, they are finding that you must pay attention to your core business.

Circuit City Stores, Inc. Though Best Buy passed Circuit City in sales in FY 1996, Circuit City rebounded to regain the sales lead in FY 1997. They held on to that lead until FY 2000. That's when Best Buy added more than 1,300 stores through acquisitions.

Sales for FY 2004 came in at $9.7 billion, down about 2 percent from FY 2003. The company had an operating loss of just over $89 million. Circuit City averaged $484 in sales per square foot of store space. Their typical store averages just over 33,000 square feet in size.

Circuit City owns and operates 604 retail stores. The CarMax retail automotive locations have been separated from Circuit City. The CarMax group is now a separately owned company. In FY 2002, Circuit City got out of the appliance business in order to focus more on their core business, consumer electronics. The company has since beefed up its video departments and added liquid crystal and plasma technologies.

In addition, the company is restructuring and retraining its sales force, revamping selected stores, and installing full-store lighting upgrades in nearly half of their locations. So while Best Buy may have won recent battles, the war isn't over yet.

Staples, Inc. Staples is a young and innovative retailer of office products. The eighteen-year-old chain now has nearly 1,500 stores worldwide. Sales for FY 2004 were $14.4 billion.

The focus of the company is to supply small and medium-sized businesses with office supplies, business machines, computers, and furniture. Their target customers include conventional corporate offices, home-based businesses, professionals, teachers, and business organizations.

Stores typically carry about 8,000 SKUs, including some 1,000 private-label consumable items. North American retail stores generate about 62 percent of the company's sales. Online efforts add another 30 percent, and European operations account for the remaining 8 percent. Staples is headquartered in Framingham, Massachusetts.

Office Depot, Inc. Office Depot was founded in 1986 and now operates 956 office products superstores. Sales for FY 2004 came in at $13.6 billion, just a few sticky notes and paper clips behind the industry leader, Staples.

Office Depot's target market includes small offices, home-based businesses, and medium-sized firms in the United States and Europe. The company has a strong global Internet presence, and generated about $2.1 billion in e-commerce sales in FY2002.

Stores carry about 7,900 SKUs including store-brand consumables. North American retail operations generate approximately 60 percent of the company's annual revenue, online sales account for nearly 19 percent of sales with the remainder coming from foreign retail operations.

Office Depot's growth, business model, and market position is very close to that of Staples. Both companies have kept a similar pace of operations for eighteen years. The next decade may produce some separation if one chain can create a sustainable market advantage.

Toys "R" Us, Inc. Things have not all been fun and games in America's largest toy store chain this past decade. The company had been a successful specialty toy retailer, but slipped to become just another commodity outlet—engaged in price wars with major discount competitors such as Wal-Mart, Target, and Kmart.

Toys "R" Us stores have aged, and price competition has reduced profit margins and net income. In the 1990s, the chain diversified by adding Kids "R" Us and Babies "R" Us stores, which branched out into apparel and furniture. The loss of focus, lack of direction, heavy borrowing, and fragmented marketing efforts nearly took the company under.

In 2000, John H. Eyler, Jr., joined the company as president and CEO. Eyler had the unenviable job of turning the struggling company back into the "powerhouse" retailer it once was. In late 2003, the company closed 182 Kids "R" Us and Imaginarium stores in order to free up resources and refocus on core-business efforts. The company began major renovations to freshen up store appearances.

In early 2005, Toys "R" Us was purchased by a group of investors for $6.6 billion. Some of the investors have significant real estate experience, and analysts anticipate that the company will close unprofitable stores, sell off some real estate, and refocus on toy retailing.

Wholesale Clubs

The "pile it deep and sell it cheap" wholesalers are still alive and well in this no-frills, high-volume, low-margin retail segment. However, the field has been narrowed to two major players: Costco and Wal-Mart's Sam's Clubs.

Between the two, they account for about $76 billion in annual revenues. Both companies target small-business owners and individuals as customers. An annual fee is required for membership.

Costco Wholesale Corporation. Costco operates an international chain of 449 warehouse stores that generate average sales per store in excess of $100 million. In FY 2004, total revenues came in at $47.1 billion, making Costco "king of the hill" in warehouse retailing.

The company offers three membership types: business, individual, and executive. Stores are generally open seven days per week for all members. Special hours are reserved for business and executive members.

Basic operations have changed little over the past decade. The company still sells a limited number of items in several broad categories, in a no-frills, no-salespeople, low-overhead environment. Costco had 42 million cardholder members in 2004.

Sam's Clubs. The Sam's Clubs stores are an operating segment of Wal-Mart Stores, Inc. This warehouse division produced $37.1 billion in revenues for FY 2005, from 551 store locations. This equates to average sales of more than $62 million per store.

Though the Sam's Club division has enjoyed steady growth since 1996, the segment has lagged behind industry leader Costco. In 1994, Sam's Club's had annual revenues of $12.3 billion, or $2.7 billion less than Costco. In FY 2003, they trailed Costco by nearly $10 billion in sales.

Sam's is a "membership only" concept that targets small-business owners and individuals. Currently more than 47 million cardholders shop at Sam's Clubs. The division is twenty-one years old, and if its sales were accounted for separately, Sam's would rank among the top twelve retail chains.

Become a David

We realize we have painted a pretty gloomy picture of the giants to this point. They are big, and some are tough to compete against. But do not despair. There is hope. Little David faced overwhelming odds when he went up against the Philistine giant Goliath. But David was armed with everything he needed. The weapons you need are in this book.

You can survive. Even if you've lost customers, you can win them back. You can prosper and grow. We know you can because we've talked with hundreds of independents just like you, and they are becoming successful competitors. They are learning how to counter the giant's strengths.

These new competitors are using the success strategies we describe in the next chapter. They are employing the tactics we've woven throughout the book. We share their stories; you can read about owners just like yourself. Owners who are becoming smarter, faster, tougher, and more focused on running profitable businesses. And they are improving their businesses, and increasing sales and profits, and some are setting all-time performance highs.

They may have had their backs to the wall, but they're no longer backing up. They are going forward with determination and vigor. They refuse to run, and they won't hide. They are armed with information. They are winning because of their positive attitudes and because they are learning how to fight. So read on, friends, gather up some new information, and reenter the battle. You can win. You can prosper and grow. We'll supply the "how to" if you'll bring the "want to."

Key Points Checklist

- ☑ The big-boxes continue to get bigger, and many independents are still struggling to compete.

- ☑ Some big-box chains have survived bankruptcy, merged with other companies, or been acquired by outside investors. Some are still struggling to compete.

- ☑ There is a new breed of small-box dollar stores with highly aggressive expansion plans that are becoming a challenge in many markets.

- ☑ Despite the competition, millions of small-business owners are thriving by doing the right things well.

- ☑ The remainder of this book is devoted to teaching you the right things to do, and how to do them well.

Fourteen Success Strategies

CHAPTER 2

The toughest thing about success is that you've got to keep on being a success.

— IRVING BERLIN

During the past two decades we have worked closely with nearly 5,000 small-business owners. As we did the research for this book, we visited with hundreds of successful owners, including most of those we interviewed for the first book back in 1994.

As we visited with these bright, hardworking men and women, it became apparent that many of them had moved from *survival* to *success*. Therefore, we have changed the "Survival Strategies" to the "Success Strategies."

If you are ready to choose success, you'll find direction in this chapter. We've distilled our research into fourteen brief operational strategies. Use these strategies to guide you toward success.

The Fourteen Success Strategies

1. It's still about the customer.

2. Great companies have great people.

3. Add obvious value.

4. Become a master marketer.

5. Eliminate waste.

6. Get accurate, timely management information.

7. Become a power nicher.

8. Focus on improvement.

9. Study the success of others.

10. Become a hands-on leader.

11. Conduct your business with integrity.

12. Take control of your attitude.

13. Be nice (to customers and employees).

14. Become results-oriented.

Success Strategies Overview

We will give you a brief overview of each of the fourteen success strategies in this chapter. You will find these key concepts discussed, detailed, exemplified, and elaborated on throughout the remainder of this book.

1. It's Still About the Customer.

All businesses, regardless of type or size, have one common reason to exist: to serve the customer. All of the successful companies we've studied appreciate and understand the worth of their customers.

While their estimates of the value of a lifetime customer vary from a few thousand dollars to more than a million dollars, they all agree that their customers are their most valuable asset. Though you'll never find the customer listed on their balance sheets as an "asset," savvy owners tell us that keeping their customers happy keeps the value in all other assets.

Every day businesses liquidate assets for pennies on the dollar of original cost. Why? Because they've forgotten the importance of their customers. We are convinced that this single factor has caused the early demise of millions of small businesses.

What Customers Want. There are reasons why millions of customers are flocking to the big-box discounters and category killers. You can learn why, and then use these reasons to your advantage. If you want to compete successfully, you must know what customers want and then position your business to give it to them.

1. *Customers want value.* Value is the relationship between price, and quality and quantity. Everyone—rich or poor—wants to get more for the money they spend. The discounters have lowered prices to create a higher perception of value. By studying their sales and growth records you can see it works.

   We view the value relationship as a seesaw. At one end of the seesaw is a heavy person named "price." On the other end are two skinny folks named "quality" and "quantity." Customers only see value when the seesaw is level. That is, when how much they have to pay (price) equals the features, benefits, and excellence (quality) and how much (or many) they get (quantity).

   Your job as a small-business owner is to add value on the quality and quantity end. In every chapter of this book, we'll provide examples of how you can create a better value relationship with every customer.

2. *Customers want convenience.* Spoken or unspoken, the customer's cry is the same: Save me time, make my life easy. Time is a commodity that is in short supply in most people's lives. We are willing to trade money for time and convenience.

   There are many examples from current life. We pay someone to do our laundry, wash our cars, clean our houses, mow our yards, cook our meals, and watch our children. We make these trade-offs because we value our time.

   Convenience, then, is all about saving your customers' time and making their lives less complicated. Here are a few examples of convenience factors: easy to access locations, parking near the store, credit card acceptance, drive-through pickup, and fast checkouts. (You'll find many more convenience factors in Chapter Four, "Keeping Customers.")

3. *Customers want service.* Unfortunately, the customers' definitions of service don't always match those of small-business owners. One of the things the big-boxes did was redefine the term *customer service.*

As we provide a few service definitions, you will see that there is a connection between "convenience" and "service." They are related. You cannot provide good service without the convenience factors.

Some examples of good service include: long open-for-business hours, clean restrooms, one-stop shopping, not having to wait in long lines at checkout, and easy return policies. (See Chapter Four, "Keeping Customers," for more on service and many more "customer-generated" service definitions.)

4. *Customers want information.* We should make a distinction here. Some customers choose to remain ignorant. Low-price buyers seem more willing to accept products at face value if the price is cheap. Since most successful competitors don't really want to deal with the low-price buyers, we'll say that discriminating customers want information.

Discriminating customers desire information for two main reasons: 1) to make correct decisions, and 2) for reassurance. Merchants who train their employees well will include "product knowledge" in their training program.

Relevant, benefit-oriented information will help customers reach the correct purchasing decision, and having the information will help reassure them that they made the right decision. Customers who buy what's right for them feel good about the purchase and the business they bought it from.

5. *Customers want choices.* There is a reason why Wal-Mart Supercenters carry 150,000 different items. It's not to confuse customers; it's to allow them the freedom of choice. Differing budgets, tastes, and needs dictate a variety of choices.

Successful competitors understand the need for carrying a good selection of products that allow the customer to find what is right for them. There is a fine line here. If you have too much inventory, you slow down the turn of merchandise and tie up valuable capital; too little, and you risk not having what the customer wants or needs.

The secret to having success in this area is knowing your customers. While you can't be everything to everybody, you have to be something special to your targeted customers.

6. *Customers want peace.* Webster defines peace as "an undisturbed state of mind; absence of mental conflict; and freedom from disagreement or quarrels." In other words, customers do not want hassles.

As a rule, people try to avoid conflict and disagreement. Most customers don't like to argue, and more often than not, customers will walk away before they complain. However, you should not assume that because you hear no complaints, all is well.

Some of the most aggravating hassle factors are: waiting in line; poor return policies; rude, argumentative staff; out-of-stock items; not having public restrooms; and no help when it's needed.

Jim and Roger Myers, owners of Jim Myers Drug, Inc., an independently owned five-store chain in Tuscaloosa, Alabama, that has achieved a nearly 20 percent growth rate for the past five years, have focused their efforts on giving the customers exactly what they want. Jim describes the service they provide to ensure that all customers are satisfied: "Giving customers what they want begins with your attitude. We take good care of our employees, and they take good care of our customers. Then we add value by offering free screening for common diseases and free delivery for prescriptions and medical equipment."

2. Great Companies Have Great People.

The companies we researched for this book unanimously agreed on one point: They could not have grown successful businesses without great people. In fact, no business ever attains a higher level of quality than the quality of people who work there.

Henry Ford, founder of Ford Motor Company, said, "You can take my factories, burn up my building, but give me my people, and I'll build the business right back again." General Robert E. Wood, former president of Sears, Roebuck & Company, said, "Put your personnel work first, because it is the most important."

Perhaps one of our small business success stories may have expressed it best. Bill Marshall, President of Phelps County Bank in Rolla, Missouri, said, "Great employees create great customers." The bank is 100 percent employee-owned, and has experienced solid growth every year for the past ten years. In fact, in all of the well-managed businesses we talked to, employees are encouraged to take initiative in helping customers. They are not only motivated to take care of customers, they are empowered to solve problems and create good feelings.

Having the *right people* in the *right job*, with the *right training, the right tools*, and *the right attitude* is a powerful competitive strategy. We are devoting all of Chapter Five to providing the information, tools, and skills you'll need to hire, motivate, and keep great people.

Ten Traits of Great Employees

Training can build skills, but it seldom changes personalities and attitudes. You must hire those. Here are some traits to look for:

1. *High Self-Esteem.* This trait is described by experts as the greatest single predictor of success in any activity. People who have it tend to take calculated risks and to be more productive than most.

   They tend to say, "If life hands you lemons, make lemonade." In contrast, when self-esteem is low, employees will spend time reading help-wanted ads and daydreaming.

2. *Good Communication Skills.* Good communicators will look you straight in the eye, volunteer information, and listen attentively, too. Jim Chick, president of Chick's Sporting Goods in Covina, California, a small chain that has grown from six stores in 1994 to eleven stores today, described the importance of this trait:

"It's very easy to give people product knowledge. That's not the hard part. The hard part is teaching them to be aggressive and to want to wait on people, communicate with people, listen to what the customer wants and try to fulfill their needs."

Chick has had success in keeping key people. His general manager has been with him thirty-six years, ten buyers and assistants average twenty-two years, and ten store managers average eighteen years. Obviously, these long-term employees communicate well with their customers and their boss.

3. *Self-Motivation.* Great people are goal-oriented, know where they want to go, and have a plan to get there. They don't have to be pushed or petted. They arrive at work early, and look for things to do when they get there.

Mac Miller, owner of American Band Instrument Service in Tyler, Texas, has achieved double-digit sales growth each of the past three years. He has an interesting philosophy in this area. He recommends, "Hire people who are already motivated."

4. *Dependability.* It's essential to find employees who possess this basic trait. Dependable people will do what they promise to do and produce work that is consistent in quality. They show up, are on time, and can be counted on.

5. *Energy and Dedication to Hard Work.* Direct Tire and Auto Service's owner Barry Steinberg, who thrives in Watertown, Massachusetts amid competition from national tire chain stores, is such a believer in the importance of this trait that he interviews prospective employees three times, at three different times of day. He's looking for people who have a high energy level throughout the day. High-energy people have allowed Steinberg to double the number of stores he operates.

6. *A Positive Attitude.* Later in this chapter, you will find that having a positive attitude is one of the Fourteen Success Strategies. It is also one of the most important predictors of success among individuals. People with positive attitudes also possess many other traits we list in this section.

Ken Dumminger, owner of Dumminger Photography in Fremont, Ohio, is a good example of the value of having a positive attitude despite negative circumstances. Two years ago Dumminger had to undergo a life-threatening liver transplant. His customers came to his rescue, and today he and his business are healthier than before. Why all the customer and community support? Positive people are the best friends that customers and communities can ever have.

7. *Perseverance.* Those with this trait will do whatever it takes, for as long as it takes. They don't quit when the going gets tough. They finish what they start. Thomas Edison would never have perfected the light bulb if he had given up after one hundred tries.

8. *Enthusiasm.* People who are genuinely enthusiastic are more likely to succeed. Their enthusiasm is their inspiration to action. Excited people talk about doing things; enthusiastic people do them. Charles Schwab said, "A man can succeed at almost anything for which he has unlimited enthusiasm."

9. *A Sense of Humor.* A person who has the ability to take work seriously, but not themselves, can be a great addition to a team.
    One college administrator we know says, "I look for a sense of humor in every interview I conduct. If a nervous candidate can make me laugh during the interview, I know there is nothing wrong with their sense of humor."

10. *Integrity.* This is another trait that is a must for your business as well as a critical individual characteristic. Even people who are dishonest themselves prefer to do business with people of integrity. Integrity is not just a part-time thing. It's not something you can employ when you need it. You can't have integrity 99 percent of the time. You either have integrity all the time or not at all. Take good care of your integrity. If you lose it, people will remember your loss forever.
    Of all the traits listed here, we believe having a positive atti-

tude and integrity are the most important. We would not hire an employee without these two traits.

3. Add Obvious Value.

Customers define value in their own ways. They weigh the quality and quantity you offer against your price. Customers make this judgment every time they shop.

The big-boxes have attempted—with some success—to tie value to low prices. Their marketing messages have been consistent through the years: You can't go anywhere else and buy for less. This is why Wal-Mart's "price rollback" ads always show a higher price being slashed into a lower price. They add to the consumer's perception of value by cutting prices.

As a result, most independent merchants now have a higher-price perception in the consumer's mind. All too often this perception is based on fact. As small business owners, you must change this perception.

We believe one of the best ways to improve your value perception is to add obvious value. The word *obvious* means "easy to see and understand." When you add value, you must be certain that your customers both know of the value you added, and understand the benefit to them.

There are five basic ways to add value and change the customer's perception:

1. *Cut your price.* This is easy. Anyone can do it. The only problem is that cutting price also reduces margin and profit. Unless you're the low-cost provider, this method can take you right out of business.

   We suggest using the variable pricing tool we provide in Chapter Nine. This tool will help you improve your value without sacrificing margins and profit.

2. *Reduce your costs.* Wal-Mart was able to operate on about half the expense that their largest competitors consumed as operating costs. They passed part of the cost savings along their customers in the form of lower prices.

We believe that most small businesses can reduce costs. It takes a concentrated effort and focus. You'll find more on this topic in Success Strategy Number Five and in Chapter Eleven.

3. *Improve quality.* Remember, value is the balance between "quality and quantity" and "price." Adding quality to your products and services can improve your value perception.

If you carry product lines that give you problems with returns, you may need to look for a supplier with higher quality. We know a lawn and garden retailer who carried a major brand of lawn sprinklers that customers returned by the dozens. He found a new line, with almost no defects and a lower price. The result: higher quality, happier customers, less hassle, and more profit.

4. *Add service.* Free delivery, free installation, free safety checks, free lessons, and free adjustment are all examples of added service. But you must make the "free service" obvious to the customer. Point it out: "Our price includes . . ."

Barry Steinberg, owner of Direct Tire and Auto Service in Watertown, Massachusetts, adds value with a free loner car program. When customers come in for a set of tires or auto repair, they don't have to sit in a waiting room for hours. They can pick up a free loner and go to work, shopping, or home. Not only is it a great value-added service, Steinberg says it is the best promotion idea he's ever had.

5. *Bundle value.* Computer manufacturers learned early on to bundle software on their computers for greater sales. Packaging products and services can certainly add value in the eye of the consumer.

A hardware owner bundles a package of wood hickory chips with every barbecue grill. A clothier bundles a shirt and tie with every suit sold. A vacuum cleaner dealership provides a free one-year service contract with all of their better vacuums.

There are many ways to add value. Ask your employees to help you come up with new ideas. And don't forget to tell the customers—it must be *obvious* to be effective. The key to success with this strategy is to find services that have a higher perceived value than your actual cost.

Greg Lair, a Canyon, Texas, automobile dealer, offers free oil changes for as long as you own the new or used car you bought from his dealership. The value perceived by the customer is several times the actual cost to the dealership. In addition to adding value, Lair feels that his "free oil change program" also offers opportunities to build lifetime relationships with his customers.

4. Become a Master Marketer.

We define marketing as every action you take to create, satisfy, and keep customers. In practice, marketing must attract new customers, completely fulfill their needs, wants, and expectations, and establish a relationship to bring them back again.

Marketing is a never-ending process that begins with making potential customers aware of your business with advertising, promotion, and personal selling. It continues with quality products and services that both satisfy your customer's needs and wants and create a perception of value. Though the process never ends, marketing has a goal of building a lasting relationship with every customer.

There are six basic components of marketing. These are often referred to as the marketing mix. We call them the six P's of marketing. They include: *price, product* (or service), *place, promotion, people,* and *positioning.* These six components, utilized in the proper relationship, are the foundation to build a growing business on. They are also the basic elements required to create an effective marketing plan.

Jerrold Taylor is an engineer by training and a master marketer by experience. So he not only knows good engineering when he sees it, he knows how to evaluate its marketing potential.

Six years ago, he and two business partners purchased a small, computerized saw manufacturing company called Monet De Sauw. Taylor said, "We found great engineering throughout the product lines. More importantly, all six of the basic marketing elements were there. They hadn't been used, but they were there."

From 1998 to 2004, the new owners grew the business from a position of being dead last in units sold among major saw manufacturers to the *number two position* in the industry. Sales during this period have increased by more than 500 percent. Taylor explains, "Even great products won't sell themselves. Marketing sells our customers their first saw; our quality and service ensure follow-up sales."

You will find a detailed discussion of the six P's of marketing in Chapter Three. We've included other relevant aspects of marketing in Chapters Four, Five, Six and Seven. We've added this powerful information because we see a direct connection between becoming a master marketer and achieving success.

5. Eliminate Waste.

Thomas Edison said, "Waste is worse than loss. The time is coming when every person who lays claim to ability will keep the question of waste before him constantly. The scope of thrift is limitless."

One of the keys to controlling waste is to plan your spending. Create an annual budget and analyze all expenses against your budget. Constant comparison of actual to budget will allow you to pick up unexpected increases early on. Then you can take immediate steps to control the waste.

The late Sam Walton, founder of Wal-Mart Stores, Inc., became the richest man in America in 1985. He learned early in his life the value of eliminating waste. Perhaps Walton studied the writings of Cicero. In 46 B.C., Cicero wrote, "Men do not realize how great an income thrift is."

Several years ago, as we started to study the Wal-Mart phenomenon, we began to track the company's operating, selling, and general and administrative expenses as a percentage of sales. The percentage has always been low, but according to their annual report, it dipped to a flat 15 percent in fiscal 1994. Contrast this to Sears and Roebuck whose operating expenses still exceed 30 percent after major cost-cutting during the last two years.

Many small-business owners carry operating expense loads of as much as 40 to 45 percent of sales. While many of these expenses are justified, others simply are not. They have become a part of the business and are as accepted as the "middle-age spread."

Unfortunately, when you're up against the Wal-Marts, there isn't any room for middle-age spread. The "big-box" merchants are young, lean, and work hard to stay in shape. Their fitness may be found in their operating expense levels and their inventory turns.

Bill Hanson, Jr., owner of two office equipment stores in the New York City metro area that have achieved sales increases of 15 percent or more each of the past three years, explains an important aspect of keeping your costs low: "If we don't manage our costs properly, we can't offer our products and services at competitive prices."

Hanson is right on target. We've seen thousands of businesses who let their costs grow without proper controls, and soon they've given away their competitive position.

For all of you who have responsibility for managing the bottom line, here are eight elements to consider when eliminating waste:

1. Remember that every dollar saved from your current operating costs goes directly to your bottom line.

2. You must justify *every expense*—every day, every month, every year.

3. You must eliminate nonessential expenses as soon as you identify them.

4. Start with an analysis of your five largest expense categories. Are you getting the maximum return for each dollar spent?

5. Remember, time is money and eliminating time wasters saves money.

6. You should carefully evaluate any inventory that turns at 50 percent or less than your overall average turns. Clear out slow-moving items unless the profit margin is high enough to justify the slow movement.

6. Get Accurate, Timely Management Information.

The new breed of big-box merchants have all invested heavily in technology. The advantage they get from their investment is management information at their fingertips. They know sales figures from yesterday, last week, and last month. They know their current level of orders in progress, inventory in transit, and inventory on the shelves. Their computers allow them to know what's going on so they can make wise decisions based on accurate, timely information.

Contrast that with many smaller independents who, for the most part, don't know their status from month to month. Many of the business owners we've worked with are still getting financial statements once a year and often they do not understand exactly what the numbers mean. By the time they get the information, most of it is out of date and is of little use other than to offer some historical perspective.

George Wilder is the owner of the Locker Room, a thriving upscale men's wear store in Montgomery, Alabama. He feels strongly about getting timely, accurate financial information. Wilder said, "I couldn't run my business without regular data from our point-of-sale system and from my bookkeeper. I belong to a buying group because it helps us maintain healthy margins."

As we interviewed candidates for our success stories, it became apparent that those who were thriving and prospering knew a lot about their businesses. For them, knowledge of their business was a top priority.

They have developed systems—sometimes manual, often automated—to monitor the following areas:

- Financial information

- Customer information

- Industry information

- Market trends and information

We detail the fundamental types of information that small businesses need and offer tips on using that data later in the book. In terms of collecting the information, there is no long-term substitute for technology. We're convinced that the business owners who are able to stand up to the new breed, will be computerized. It will take commitment, capital, and time. However, the benefits will outweigh the effort many times over.

7. Become a Power Nicher.

The big-boxes have become successful as mass merchandisers. They carry large selections that appeal to wide audiences. By trying to have something for everyone, they leave hundreds of retail and service gaps that we refer to as niches.

By definition a niche is "a place or position that is particularly well suited to the person or thing in it." In business, becoming a power nicher means locating an area or areas where your unique abilities, skills, and offerings match the needs and wants of your customers. Power niching means capitalizing on those areas where your business can excel.

For Aledia Hunt Tush, owner of CB's Saltwater Outfitters on Siesta Key near Sarasota, Florida, the power niche is knowing the local fishing and boating conditions, using up-to-date fishing information to sell what works, and knowledge and experience to make every outing a success. Wal-Mart may carry hundreds of items not found at Mr. CB's, but they can't tell you where or how to catch fish or rent you a boat to enjoy a day on the water.

For Betty Roberts, owner of Focus on Fashion, an upscale ladies-wear shop in Montgomery, Alabama, the power niche is making women look and feel good. Roberts and co-owner Dale Gulledge help their customers select flattering styles and colors, match accessories to go with them, and create wardrobes that are versatile and professional. Wal-Mart may carry thousands of clothing items you'll never find at Focus on Fashion, but they can't help their customers gain the self-confidence that comes with looking great and knowing it!

For Ruth Hanessian, president of the Animal Exchange, a pet store in Rockville, Maryland, the power niche is providing the highest quality in pet care and supplies and a total commitment to helping owners enjoy healthy, responsive, and long-lived pets. Wal-Mart may sell bigger bags of dog food for less, but they'll never call you or your puppy or kitty by name, and they won't help you raise a healthier, happier pet.

8. Focus on Improvement.

A small-business owner once told us he had read our first book and had committed to change. We applauded his efforts, but afterward wondered if that owner realized that change and improvement are two different words.

While change is necessary to improve, improvement does not always follow change. For example, you could replace your modern bathroom with a primitive outhouse and achieve a major change, but no improvement.

The Japanese have a word for their informal Total Quality Management process. The word is *Kaizen* (*Ky'zen*). Kaizen means "continuous improvement involving everyone."

The successful business owners we interviewed as we did research for this book are practicing Kaizen whether or not they knew the word. They know their future business depends on how well they managed their last opportunity to satisfy their customer. If the last experience was a positive one for your customers, they'll come back. If it wasn't, they will find another supplier for the products or services they've been buying from you.

Bill Hanson, Jr., mentioned earlier in this chapter, who owns Office Systems, Inc., is a believer in continuous improvement. His industry is one that doesn't stand still. Bill says, "Our industry is technology, and technology changes quickly. We must be on top of our game or risk obsolescence."

We've dedicated all of Chapter Eleven to helping you understand the Kaizen theory and giving you a list of thought starters. Use this list to find a few areas to begin improving. Get your employees involved. We don't believe you'll find it difficult to find something to improve.

9. Study the Success of Others.

It's simplistic, but true: If you want to be a smart business person, study smart businesses. All of the successful companies we studied for this book have learned from the good business practices of others. The smart ones ask a lot of questions, keep their eyes wide open, and adapt good ideas whenever they can.

You can steal good ideas from many sources and change them to suit your situation. Three of the best sources are your competitors, your peers, and everyone else.

Study the Competition. Today's successful owners are constantly learning about and from their competition. If you're faced with stiff competition from Wal-Mart, Walgreens, or Home Depot, find out more about them.

Sam Walton studied his competitors. He read their annual reports and spent time in their stores. He observed, he borrowed, he adapted, and he succeeded.

To learn about your competitors, study all published information. Review their annual reports, SEC 10-K filings, and industry evaluations. Call a librarian or stockbroker for specifics.

Remember to visit competitors' stores. Look at the way they merchandise different departments; see what they display in high traffic areas and near the checkout areas. Observe the type of customer who is shopping there. Yogi Berra said, "You can see a lot just by looking around."

Learn from Your Peers. Join or become active in a trade association for your industry. Attend markets, buying shows, and trade meetings. Ask questions, take notes, and listen. Most successful owners use these techniques.

They also take time to visit merchants in other parts of the country. By viewing the operations of others, they gather great ideas for merchandising, promotions, purchasing sources, and pricing.

When coauthor Don Taylor was in the lawn and garden business, he once visited a fellow Snapper mower dealer in the Kansas City, Missouri, area. This high-volume dealer displayed a Snapper riding mower standing up. He showed Don how easy it was to point out the unit's simple features this way. In addition, the display required less space, which freed up space for other products.

Gather Good Ideas from Everyone. Not all good ideas come from competitors and merchants in your industry. Every person you know is a source of good business ideas. Your clergyman, your barber or hairdresser, unrelated business owners, and customers are all potential idea people.

Your employees are a great source of ideas. They are customers of many different businesses, and with proper incentive; they will be on the lookout for great ideas wherever they shop.

You must adapt a mind-set wherein you consider every situation you encounter as an opportunity to gather ideas to use in your business. When you're looking for ideas, they will come. When they do, steal like a burglar and soak up like a sponge. Adapt those ideas, and make them your own.

10. Become a "Hands-on" Leader.

We once asked a good friend and customer why he stopped doing business with a particular business. He replied, "The owner left the business to the kids."

We said that we were surprised that the owner had retired, and didn't realize that he had children to leave the business to. "Oh, he didn't retire," our friend explained, "And he doesn't have children of his own. He's just never at the business. He lets the kids that work for him run the business. I just got tired of dealing with the kids."

It's a common situation among small-business owners. They work hard, achieve some success, and then take more and more time off. They, in essence, become absentee owners.

For a while the business may function reasonably well. But we've watched the gradual deterioration of enough once well-run businesses to know that no one will run your business as well as you can, and no one will care more about your customers than you do.

There are always reasons for the success of any business, and "hands on" leadership is one of them. Billionaire Warren Buffett built the financial powerhouse Berkshire-Hathaway with a hands-on philosophy. He says, "A manager must care intensely about running a first-class operation; if his golf game is what he thinks about while shaving, the business will show it."

Wal-Mart founder Sam Walton built the largest retail company in the world with "hands-on" involvement. In his autobiography, *Made in America,* Walton listed his rules for business success. Rule One is: *Commit to your business.* Walton said, "If you love your work, you'll be out there every day trying to do it the best you possibly can, and pretty soon everybody around will catch the passion from you—like a fever." If "hands-on" leadership, commitment, and management worked for Warren Buffett and Sam Walton, it will work for you. Go to work, and make it work.

11. Conduct Your Business with Integrity.

There is no foundation for success as solid and secure as integrity. Businesses are built on relationships, and relationships are built on trust. Nothing inspires trust more thoroughly than a lifetime of honesty and integrity.

Integrity creates happy customers, partners, vendors, suppliers, employees, bosses, and families. Integrity is one of the characteristics most admired in great leaders. Integrity is a trait most desired among friends.

The quality of integrity is often defined as "acting on sound moral principles, " "dealing with honesty and sincerity," and, more recently, "avoiding spin, white lies, and strategic omissions." We must not only think the truth, act the truth, and speak the truth, but we must also consider the impact of not being truthful. Thomas Jefferson said, "Honesty is the first chapter of wisdom."

Don Griffin, owner of West L.A. Music in Los Angeles, credits his consistent growth in sales and profits to two factors: "We provide great customer service, and we deal with every customer with 100 percent integrity. Maybe that's why sales are up more than 30 percent over the past two years, and some of the West Coast's biggest music stars are regular customers at West L.A. Music."

The bottom line is that people do business with people they like and trust. Integrity builds trust, and trust is necessary for all relationships to grow and prosper. For Lee Sherman, owner of Hahn Appliance Center in Tulsa, Oklahoma, integrity is more than a buzzword or catchphrase. Sherman said, "We sell honesty, ethics, service, and value. Nothing in our business is as important as our integrity and honesty. We have had eleven big-box competitors enter our trade area in the past ten years. Our integrity is one of the competitive advantages that has kept us in business."

When you're faced with decisions that impact your integrity, ask yourself these questions: Is it legal? Is it fair to all involved? Would I be proud if this situation were to appear on the front page of tomorrow's paper?

12. Take Control of Your Attitude.

Attitude is the state of mind with which we approach any given situation. When the competition seems unbeatable, your employees grow unbearable, and the customer becomes unsatisfiable, remember this: You are still in charge of your own attitude.

We may sound like motivational speakers here, but the fact remains that every successful business owner we've talked to has kept a positive attitude despite negative circumstances. Many have overcome great difficulties, and risen from the depths of despair to the pinnacle of success because of their attitudes.

Best-selling author Zig Ziglar has said, "It's your attitude that determines your altitude." We agree, and would quickly add that your attitude also determines your latitude and longitude. In other words, how *high* and how *far* you go in this world is dependant on the attitude you take to work every day.

The key to success in this area is to take control of your attitude. No one can make you have a bad day unless you allow them to.

Debbie Kramer, owner of Kari Lyn's Formal and Bridal Boutique in McPherson, Kansas, understands the importance of maintaining a positive attitude. Kramer says, "Don't be in the business unless you love it. Your attitude will come across to your customers and have an overall negative effect on your business." We agree wholeheartedly. When you take control of your attitude and become positive, your customers will notice, your employees will see it, and every problem becomes less of a challenge.

Author and evangelist Charles R. Swindoll said, "Words can never adequately convey the incredible impact of our attitude toward life. The longer I live, the more convinced I become that life is 10 percent what happens to us and 90 percent how we respond to it."

We have found that those business owners who believe they can succeed are correct. Unfortunately, those who believe they cannot are also correct.

You get to choose your attitude. Take control, choose to be positive, and choose to make the changes in your business that will make you more successful than you've ever been.

13. Be Nice.

One of the great joys of writing a book like this is that you get to meet a lot of really nice people. It is one of the common factors we've found among our success stories; these men and women are truly nice folks.

Contrary to the old saying, "Nice guys finish last," we've found the nice factor carries folks to the top. It's a common trait among winners.

In *How to Think Like a CEO*, author D. A. Benton found twenty-two vital traits that had carried CEOs to the top of their companies. One of those traits was that CEOs were nice.

Being nice doesn't mean that you are weak or let others push you around. It doesn't mean that you can't get results or make tough decisions. Being nice means that you respect other people and their needs, feelings, and situations. It means being friendly, interested, and fair.

Jack McNabb, owner of Trenton Hardware in Trenton, Missouri, sums up his entire business philosophy in two words: *Be nice.*

Your mother gave you great advice all those times when she scolded you and said, "Be nice!" *Being nice is a highly underutilized technique for growing your business, improving your relationships, and enjoying your life.*

14. Become Results-Oriented.

Beware of the activity trap. Sometimes folks who seem to be busy all the time get very little done. They often become victims of the activity trap. They confuse activity (doing something) with productivity (getting results). Checking your e-mail, returning phone calls, and writing memos may burn up several hours each day without anything important being accomplished. It is easy to choose the urgent over the important.

One of the key factors we found among the successful entrepreneurs we've worked with is that they are more interested in results than hard work. This doesn't mean that they aren't hard workers—they are—it just means that they have come to realize that working smart is equally important as working hard.

Becoming results-oriented means that you begin to direct your activities toward those things that will produce the outcomes you want to achieve.

Obviously, this means that you must have a clear idea of the results you want before you start. Another way of saying this is to begin with the end in mind. First, determine what you want, and then work toward those objectives.

Key Points Checklist

☑ Success is a choice.

☑ Success is achieved by those who try.

☑ Success is achieved through the relentless pursuit of doing simple things well. The Fourteen Success Strategies are some of the simple things you'll have to do well to be successful.

☑ Compare your operation to the common success strategies. Work on those areas where you have voids or weaknesses.

☑ Other areas in this book will help you find ways to improve in any of the Fourteen Success Strategies where you need help.

Creating Customers

CHAPTER 3

Customers are good for business.

—Len Baker

According to Greek legend, King Midas was granted the power to turn everything he touched into gold. The successful competitors that we have included in this book have found that marketing is their "Midas touch."

They have discovered that a thorough understanding and effective application of basic marketing principles will help attract new customers and turn them into golden long-term profits. Our friend and colleague, Len Baker, is right—customers are good for business!

Wal-Mart and other mega-merchants spend billions of dollars every year on marketing and promotion. They, too, know that customers are good for business.

As a small-business owner, you don't have millions, let alone billions of dollars to spend. Do not despair. We've talked to owners who are having solid, effective marketing success, and they only spend a few thousand dollars per year to execute their plans. By using the marketing, promotion, and selling tactics that we've packed into this chapter and the three that follow, you can become more successful too.

Marketing Defined

Our definition of marketing won't be found in any marketing textbook. It's not theory; it's not supposition; it's been proven on Main

Streets across the nation. We define marketing as "every action you take to *create, satisfy,* and *keep* customers." By *create,* we mean to attract customers and inspire them to do business with you. By *satisfy,* we mean the complete fulfillment of each customer's needs, desires, and expectations. By *keep,* we mean the development of a relationship so strong that you are always your customer's first choice.

This chapter will focus on the first phase of marketing—attracting customers. Chapter Four will zero in on turning onetime buyers into lifetime customers—the satisfying and keeping phases.

The Six P's of the Marketing Mix

There are six basic elements that dictate overall marketing success. These key elements are often referred to as the marketing mix. They are *price, product* (or *service*), *place, promotion, people,* and *positioning.*

We have never seen a successful marketing plan that didn't include all six elements. Some may be executed better than others, but all six are there. In the brief discussions below, we will try to show you how each element depends on all the others in order to create a seamless marketing strategy.

The Price Factor

Price is the first of the elements and one of the most critical. Every person who has an average IQ or even a lick of common sense wants to purchase the highest quality and the largest quantity, at the lowest price.

Although not all products are price-sensitive (visible), usually the price is more visible than the quality. For example, we may be considering the purchase of a compact stereo unit. One unit may sell for $500 and another for $300. Since both look similar, have nearly identical features, sound alike, and make the same advertising claims, we might assume that the quality is the same. However, we've heard for years "that we get just what we pay for," so we are conditioned to believe that the more expensive model must be better.

The point here is that most of us cannot tell the quality of a stereo from looks, sound, or brand name alone. So when we perceive little, if any, quality differential, we'll go for low price every time.

The Product Factor

The product element is one of the most critical in your mix. If the product element is off, you won't have anything to sell that your customers want to buy. Therefore, you don't have any reason to be in the marketplace. This is why many small businesses are either barely hanging on or going out of business.

Regardless of the level of service you provide and the low, low price you offer, the product must be wanted or needed. Whether you are dealing with a tangible product such as hardware, or an intangible product such as computer repair, there must be demand for what you are selling.

We have found that businesses that are successful in the product area realize that customers are buying more of their business than just the product. Here is a shortlist of what customers are really buying:

- *They are buying you*: Your personality, your appearance, your sense of humor, and your friendly nature.

- *They are buying your service*: The way they are greeted, treated, thanked, and rewarded.

- *They are buying your reputation*: Your trustworthiness and your integrity.

- *They are buying your appearance and ambience*: How your business looks, smells, feels, and is organized.

- *They are buying your success and status*: How you are perceived in your community.

- *They are buying your entire package.*

The Place Factor

If you operate a business where the customer must come to you, having the right site may be the difference between long-term survival and early failure. Great locations have kept poorly run businesses in operation for years, while well-managed ventures have struggled due to poor site selection.

Mac Miller, owner of a fast-growing music retail and service business in Tyler, Texas, learned the value of a great location when he relocated his store to a larger building in a strong retail environment. Miller said, "Within two years our sales were up over 20 percent. In addition, our new store is much more convenient to find, so we're attracting new customers every day. We have been amazed at the increase in walk-in traffic, which has turned into large increases in small-ticket, high-margin items."

Picking the right location is not an exact science, but you can learn from the experiences of others. The late Sam Walton picked out early potential store locations from the air. He studied traffic flows and building patterns for the towns they were considering. Wal-Mart's success in picking the right locations was based on locating their stores to serve a trade area. Walton knew that if people had to drive close to or right by his store on the way into downtown, they might stop to see what Wal-Mart was all about.

As you evaluate your location, consider items such as, actual traffic counts, proximity to competitors, construction trends (growth patterns), cost of land or space, zoning restrictions, tax abatement potential, and insurance costs. There is an old adage that applies to selecting a location: "Decide in haste, repent in leisure."

The Promotion Factor

Operating a business without proper promotion is like a young man winking at a young lady in the dark. He knows what he's doing, but no one else does. All businesses, large or small, home-based or at the mall, cash-rich or up against the wall, can gain customers from good promotion.

We don't believe you have to spend a fortune to grow your business. In fact, we've found more than one hundred ways to promote your business for next to nothing. These shoestring strategies work because they are focused on the customer. (We have placed all these low-cost promotion strategies into Chapter Seven.)

The main purpose of all promotion is to get the right message, to the right person, at the right time. We refer to these as the three R's of promotion—Right message, Right audience, and Right time.

Like the six "P's" of the marketing mix, the three R's are basic but necessary. Wal-Mart spends little of their promotion budget on promoting big sale items. Instead they continually hammer home the "best quality at the lowest price" message to their target market.

Wal-Mart has proven that you don't have to spend a lot to have effective promotions. While most large retailers spend 2 to 3 percent of sales on advertising and promotion, Wal-Mart spends less than 1 percent.

They can spend less because they have the right products, the right price, and they are in the right place to serve their customers effectively. Wal-Mart uses the final two elements in the mix, people and positioning, to round out their marketing efforts.

The People Factor

Another important spoke in your marketing wheel are the people who work with you in your business. Whether you call them employees, coworkers, or associates, good people add to the value perception of your business. That is, if they are friendly, well-trained, and customer-focused.

If you truly want to distinguish your business from the megastores, people can make the difference. The successful businesses we researched are people-smart. They pay above-average wages, teach in-depth product knowledge, build customer-service skills, and provide a challenging environment to work in. They empower their employees to solve customer problems and make independent decisions.

Dwight Horne, co-owner of Clinton Appliance and Furniture in Clinton, North Carolina, sums up this point. Horne says, "We couldn't run this place without good people. Our goal is to be the friendliest store in our market area."

We have devoted all of Chapter Five to helping you find, motivate, and keep quality employees. Other small-business owners do it every day, and we know you can too. Don't forget to factor your associates into your marketing mix.

The Positioning Factor

Positioning is the art of locating a niche that matches customer needs with the unique skills and abilities of the business owner and associates. It is finding a place or position where you can excel.

Positioning is also the image of your business you create in the minds of your potential customers. Your goal is to create a unique, positive picture in your prospects' minds. Positioning separates your business from all others. It differentiates your uniqueness and benefits from all others. How you place yourself in the mind of the customer is critical.

Every business has a market position or image. Paying close attention to all factors relating to your marketing mix can take pressure off any single factor. For example, you may be able to skimp a little on the quality (provide less product) if you keep the price low. You may be able to reduce promotion costs if you are located conveniently and provide good value.

Jim Baum, a Morris, Illinois, women's fashion retailer, owns the oldest family-operated store in the state. When discussing his promotion strategy, Baum said, "Most of the things that worked before no longer work." Baum has kept his marketing plan effective by making changes and trying new things. Baum uses radio, newspaper, and direct mail for promotion, and now feels that his best return for his advertising dollars is with direct mail.

Building a Marketing Plan

To paraphrase a line from *Alice in Wonderland*: If you don't know where you want to go, any road will take you there. The same is true in business. Know where you are going, and you can build the road that will take you there. A good marketing plan can serve as your road map to creating customers.

Good planning always contains three components: (1) Assessing where are we now, (2) Deciding where we want to go, and (3) Determining the steps we must take to get from where we are to where we want to be. Your marketing plan should be a constantly evolving part of your business, so review and revise it frequently.

Before you devote any effort to creating an effective marketing plan, answer the following twelve questions. They will help you assess your strengths and weaknesses as related to marketing.

1. *Do you have products and services that customers need or want?* For any product, service, or line to sell successfully, there must be demand. Remember that "products" are one of the six key elements of marketing success.

   Since products can be either tangible goods or services, you must view everything you offer the customer as products. Every good or service should be evaluated periodically to determine its current viability.

   One of the best ways to find out what customers really want is to ask them. Maintaining a running dialogue with your customers will keep you informed of what they are thinking.

2. *Are we selling them at a price that equates to real value in the customer's mind?* The customer's perception is all that matters here. If the customer believes your price is too high, it's too high.

   Small-business owners often get whipped by the big-boxes in this area. Wal-Mart has had the same marketing message for forty-three years: "We have lower prices." Though they have said it in many ways, and though it's not always true on all items, the message has been consistent, and consumers have been conditioned to expect lower prices at the big-boxes.

   Independent-business owners must work harder at changing the value perception. Using variable pricing options, low-price guarantees, and value-added strategies, many small-business owners are changing that perception and building their customer base.

   Interestingly, two retail appliance dealers from towns named Clinton told us that the best competitive move they ever made was offering a "guaranteed low price."

   Thelma Decker, owner of T and M Appliance in Clinton,

Missouri, and Dwight Horne of Clinton Appliance and Furniture in Clinton, North Carolina, use "low price guarantees" to reassure customers that they can't go anywhere else and buy it for less.

Decker told us how she uses the guarantee. "We train our sales staff to casually mention the guarantee," she said. "Usually the customers are surprised, and with the low-price reassurance they almost always buy from us without even checking the competition. It has really helped our perception of value."

3. *Is your location convenient and attractive to your customers?* This is the *place* element of marketing. While this may be the hardest area to make complete changes in, you still only get one opportunity to make a good first impression.

We know you can't just pick your building up and move it to another location, nor can you change the basic configuration without major expense. However, we have seen some tremendous improvements made by owners who realized that their first impressions weren't good ones. A fresh coat of paint, an updated sign, a new façade, or just keeping the weeds from growing in your sidewalk can help.

Your inside appearance must also be consistent with the position you've established for your business. For example, if you have chosen to compete by offering upscale products and services, you need to look the part. If you look like a discount store, your customers will expect discount prices.

4. *Are your front-line people knowledgeable, friendly, and well-trained?* The *people* portion of marketing is a great area to distinguish your business from the big-boxes.

It is important that you take advantage of your successful promotions with great service when the customer actually comes to your business ready to buy. It's a double waste when your promotion works, but your contact people don't. You've not only wasted your promotion dollars, but you've also squandered an opportunity to turn a onetime buyer into a lifetime customer.

The best way to ensure that you have the right people working with your customers is to hire the right people in the first place. We've seen far too many small-business owners who were quick to hire and slow to fire. We've devoted all of Chapter Five to this critical topic.

5. *What business are you really in?* Give this one some thought. A bookstore does not just sell books. They market information, inspiration, knowledge, and entertainment. A hardware store does not just sell tools and parts; it sells the solution to problems and easier living. A clothing store doesn't just sell clothes; it sells an improved personal appearance, higher self-esteem, and greater self-confidence.

Knowing what you really provide to your customers will help you create a working marketing plan. Try to think of your business in terms of what benefit the customer receives when they do business with you.

6. *Who are your customers now, and why are they doing business with you?* Start by defining your customers. How closely can you describe your present customers by age, gender, geographic location, occupation, income level, marital status, family size, education, lifestyle, most common payment method, hobbies, interests, and leisure activities? Your description of your customers should be so thorough that you could spot a likely target on the street.

There are many reasons why your present customers are doing business with you. A few of the main ones are: Your open-for-business hours, the offers you make, the atmosphere you create inside and outside your business, how you treat your customers, the value perception you've created, the inventory you carry, and the convenience you offer.

Notice that all of the reasons are included in the six Ps of marketing we discussed earlier. (*Product, Price, Position, Promotion, Place,* and *People.*)

7. *What can you do to add value to the products you sell?* You learned in Chapter Two that adding obvious value was one of the key

success strategies used by the successful companies we've researched for this book.

How do you add value? By excelling in this area. Jim Myers of Jim Myers Drug in Tuscaloosa, Alabama, has grown his business from two to five locations despite fierce big-box competition. Myers said, "We add value with low-cost services that we give to our customers for free. For example, free delivery on all prescription and medical equipment. We provide free screenings for blood pressure, glucose, and cholesterol. Customers really appreciate these services, and they add a lot to our value perception."

Promote the products and services you offer that will provide added value, such as: in-store financing, an extended service policy, no-hassle return policies, a toll-free number, free delivery, a frequent buyer plan, or an excellent service department. How will your customers know of the value you add if you don't tell them?

8. *How can you reach your target customers?* Start with question six. If you don't know who your customers are, you won't be very effective in taking your marketing messages to them. You'll find more than one hundred low-cost methods for attracting customers in Chapter Seven. Some of them are sure to work with your target customers.

The successful competitors we've surveyed have used dozens of methods and mediums for reaching new customers. They told us that they get their best results from direct mail, newspapers, special events, and cable TV—in that order.

9. *How much money can you invest, and how often?* It's an old adage, but a true one, that "you have to spend money to make money," and it's never more true than in setting your advertising budget. When times get hard, everyone looks for ways to cut expenses. It's a perfectly natural reaction. One of the first things on the chopping block is often the advertising budget. Bad idea.

If necessary, find other ways to trim the budget, but use extreme caution when making cuts in advertising. Advertising is always a necessity, but it is even more important when business is slow and your customers aren't exactly beating a path to your door. Don't even think of your promotional budget as an expense. *Think of your promotion dollars as an investment in future business.* Strive to establish a generous but realistic budget.

One of the questions we're asked most often is, "How much should I spend on advertising?" We have created a new self-help tool to enable you to establish a working range for your promotion spending. It's called the Promotion Spending Guide.

You'll find the guide in Chapter Nine, along with other tools to help you compete at a higher level. The Promotion Spending Guide will help you analyze your current business condition and practices, your promotion efforts, your competitors, your local media, and your trade area, and then determine a range for promotion spending.

10. *Who are your competitors?* Anyone who is trying to attract the same "dollar" as you are is your competitor. List your competitors by name. What are their strengths and weaknesses? Research your competition by visiting their stores. Know what they are selling, what type of customers are in their stores, and what prices they're charging for the same merchandise that you sell.

Watch what your competitors like Wal-Mart are offering. Beyond the "everyday low price" that they're touting, they offer a wealth of marketing ideas that can work for even the smallest businesses. You just have to know what to look for. They have greeters who meet you at the door with a smile and a warm welcome. The shopping carts they offer will make it easy to buy in large quantities. Their large, easy-to-read signs direct you to the area you're looking for. If you pay by check or credit card, they'll make it a point to call you by name when they say their final thank-you.

These things are not done accidentally. Wal-Mart knows that people love to be acknowledged, that people who take carts tend to buy more, and that we all love to hear the sound of our own names.

11. *Why should anyone buy from you instead of your competitors?* What advantages do you have over the competition? What makes you unique? What benefits do you offer for doing business with you? If you don't have clear, concise answers to these questions, your customers may not be able to see any reasons to do business with you.

Look at all the things that make you different from your competitors. Analyze these differences to see if they offer your customers benefits that save them time or money, make their lives easier, more fun, healthier, more exciting, tastier, safer, or more satisfying. Focus your marketing plan on what you give the customer that no one else can.

These areas where you excel should become the focal point of your promotion activities. Customers need to be reminded often of the reasons doing business with you is in their own best interest. Focus on the benefits and advantages.

12. *Are there any trends or new products that might change the nature of your business?* As we write this, gas prices have climbed to record highs. Automobile dealers are suddenly finding their lots filled with big cars and SUVs as fuel-conscious consumers move to more efficient transportation. While most trends aren't this noticeable or this fast, they can be equally problematic in nature. The competitors we've included in this book have been watching trends for many years and have learned to adapt to the changes that shifting trends bring. You can stay ahead of the trends by attending your industry's conferences and conventions where industry happenings are discussed.

Building Your Customer Base

Once you have answered the questions above, you will have a thorough knowledge of your customers and their needs. You will find that you can build your business in several ways.

Seven ways to build your business:

1. *By Adding New Products, Product Lines, or Services.* When you analyze your product offerings, you may find some gaps. New products and lines can bring new customers to your business. They will not only buy your new lines, but your existing inventory as well. You may also benefit by increasing sales to your existing customers as they purchase the new products or services in addition to what they have already been purchasing from you.

2. *By Getting More Business from Your Existing Customers.* The more you know about your present customers, the better you can serve them. When you know their needs, you can point out products uniquely suited to them, you can suggest "go-with" items, and you can emphasize the benefits they will get from a particular product or service.

3. *By Attracting New Customers Like Your Best Customers Now.* Who are your best customers now? When you can identify your best customers in terms of common demographics, you position yourself to attract others just like them. One observant business owner told us that when he analyzed his best customers, he found that most of them came from one zip code. A concentrated direct mail effort netted several new customers from that area over the next twelve months.

4. *By Taking Customers Away from Your Competitors.* Let's face it; all customers—including yours—are fair game. No business "owns" any customer. When you know your competition, you can capitalize on their weaknesses and provide their customers a better business option.

5. *By Cultivating Your Most Difficult Customers.* Tough customers keep you on your toes. They sharpen your service skills and make you stretch to new limits. Difficult customers force improvement and push you to higher levels of excellence.

6. *By Focusing Your Best Efforts on Your Most Important Customers.* There's an old rule that says 20 percent of your customers produce 80 percent of your sales. Recently, one of our clients ran the numbers for himself. He found that the top 20 percent of his customers were producing 83 percent of his revenues and nearly 80 percent of his net income. He is now taking better care of his best customers.

7. *By Buying Out a Competitor.* Sometimes the best way to acquire market share is to buy it. While this is an extreme way to build your business, it can work. One business owner we know bought out a low-priced competitor, stabilized prices, and paid for the newly acquired business from increased margins.

Seven Serious Signs

When we have worked with companies to improve their performance, we can usually tell when their marketing efforts aren't working well. No matter what the management team tells us, if we see the following signs, we know we've got a lot of work to do.

1. The business lacks customer focus. For example, the "open-for-business-hours" are those the owner wants to work, not necessarily what the customer needs. Or, the owner spends more time waiting on the golf course than waiting on customers.

2. The business knows very little about its customers, and has no clear description of its target customers.

3. The business has no proven methods for reaching its target customers. Promotion usually becomes the "shotgun" approach, or business is done with the media sales person who shows up first.

4. The business knows little about its competitors, or doesn't understand that a competitor is anyone who is going after the same consumer dollar.

5. The business cannot identify a competitive position. A competitive position is an area where you can serve the customers better than anyone else.

6. The company is slow to take advantage of marketing opportunities, including marketing with technology.

7. The company thinks of marketing as "selling and advertising," and ignores the *product*, *price*, *position*, *people*, and *place* components of an effective marketing plan.

If any of these signs are visible in your current operation, you need to develop a plan aimed at creating customers. Once you develop your marketing plan, it cannot stay the same from year to year. You need new ideas and fresh thinking.

Key Points Checklist

☑ Marketing is every action you take to create, satisfy, and keep customers.

☑ The basic elements of marketing are: Price, Product, Place, Promotion, People, and Positioning.

☑ The main purpose of promotion is to get the right message to the right people at the right time.

☑ It is impossible to create an effective marketing plan if you don't know your customers, your competition, the elements of the marketing mix, and industry trends.

CHAPTER 4

Keeping Customers

Every company's greatest assets are its customers, because without customers there is no company.

—MICHAEL LEBOEUF

This chapter covers one critical topic: how to turn onetime buyers into lifetime customers. As you use the marketing strategies from Chapter Three, you will find new people who are willing to do business with you. The goal of customer service is to keep the customer who has discovered your business coming back again and again. When your marketing works, you create new customers, when your service works, you keep them coming back.

One of the most common mistakes that a business can make is to forget why it exists . . . to serve the customer. Without customers there simply is no reason for your company to stay in business. Yet many businesses seem to have lost sight of the value of customers as *individuals*, and employees have become too busy, too scarce, or too indifferent to give customers much attention.

Customers want more than just a transaction, they want someone to care about them and help them solve their problems. They want someone who offers not just an item, a thing, but who also offers knowledge, concern, and attention. Smart business owners utilize that information to look upon each customer transaction as not just a one-time event, but as an opportunity to build a long-term relationship.

The good news is that small-business owners like you are much better positioned to give customers the kind of service they are seeking and to build that type of relationship. When your customers have so many choices about where and how they spend their time and money, it's crucial to the success of your business to provide not just good service, but the kind of service that will keep them coming back again and again. Your service must add value for the customer so they will choose your business as their best option.

These Basic Truths Apply

Before we discuss the lifetime value of customers, we want to give you some fascinating new definitions of service, and share some important steps for improving your service. We need to share some truths about customers and customer service. Keep these truths in mind as you explore the remainder of this chapter.

- The quality of service that customers get directly affects their willingness to do business with you.

- Most people will pay a premium for good customer service.

- Customers who have had pleasant shopping experiences are much more likely to buy again, so your marketing costs will be lower.

- It costs five times as much to gain a new customer as it does to keep an existing customer coming back.

- Service is the difference between selling something and creating a customer. As costs skyrocket and profit margins dwindle, loyal customers will keep you in business.

- Satisfied customers will tell their friends, so you can spend less on advertising.

- Some experts estimate that businesses lose as much as 30 percent of their potential revenue because of poor customer service.

- The number one reason why customers quit doing business with any company is poor service.

What Are "Lifetime" Customers Worth?

The value of a loyal, lifetime customer can range from a few thousand dollars to hundreds of thousands. For example, consider the family of four who spends $100 each week on groceries. If that family remained loyal to one store for forty years, they would spend more than $200,000 in total sales.

Consider this example. A Dallas Cadillac dealer estimates that its average customer trades for a new car every three years. He assumes a $30,000 average sale of both the new car and the trade-in. Over a forty-year period (first purchase at age 30, last purchase at age 70) a customer will purchase thirteen vehicles at a total cost of $390,000. Remember, some folks trade every year, and own multiple cars. Some customers may buy a half a million dollars' worth of cars in their lifetime.

We know a residential builder who has built seven homes for one family. He built two for the grandparents (the original customer), two for their children, and three for the grandkids. Using an average cost of $200,000 per home, you have a customer value of $1.4 million.

So what's your customer worth? You may not sell houses, cars, or groceries, but you can use the three examples above to estimate the value of your customers. Just estimate the average sale in dollars, the average frequency in times per year, and assume a number of years. For example, a $10 average sale, times a frequency of once a week (fifty-two sales per year), times a ten year period, equals a $5,200 customer value ($10 x 52 visits, x 10 years = $5,200).

The small-business owners we surveyed for this book estimated the lifetime value of their customers in a range of $5,000 (lowest) to $1 million (highest.) Remember, these are small, independent businesses just like yours.

Now you begin to understand why every customer, and every customer contact is important. When it comes to service, every moment is a defining moment.

In a recent survey, we asked customers to think about a business they liked to trade with. Then we asked them to list the reasons why they enjoyed the experience. The quality of customer service showed up on every survey. In that same survey we asked customers to define customer service and give us some specific examples. The results are fascinating. We'll share their responses later in this chapter.

How Business Owners Define Service

As part of our research for this book, we asked every successful business owner we interviewed to complete a six-page written survey. One of the questions asked was, "How do you define the service you provide?"

As we began to analyze the answers, we were surprised that only ten words were used to define all of the owners' definitions. Here are those ten words in the order of number of mentions:

1. Personal

2. Friendly

3. Fast

4. Helpful

5. Informative

6. Honest

7. –10. Best, Great, Excellent, and Caring. (Items 7–10 received the same number of mentions.)

Of course, these are all very common answers when you quiz small-business owners about their service. What really surprised us was the contrast between what the owners said and what the customers said.

We believe that nearly all business owners overrate their level of service. They feel they offer top-quality service every day. No one can match their personal, friendly, fast, helpful, service. Perhaps it's time for a wake-up call. Before you break your arm patting yourself on the back on your great service, read the rest of this chapter to see what your customers consider important. Then sit down with your key staff people and evaluate your service compared to what the customer is really looking for.

A New Definition of Service

The definition of service is changing. While the big-box competitors have played a part in the redefining, it is the customer who has established the new definition.

For nearly two decades, coauthor Don Taylor has traveled extensively, teaching small-business owners how to be better competitors. Customer service is always a topic he spends some time on. For more than ten years he has used the following definition for service: *"Customer service is every action a business takes that enhances their customers' satisfaction with the business."*

More recently he has added the following: *"Customer service is everything a business does that increases their customers' perception of value in the products and/or services they offer."*

Two key points from those definitions are "customers' satisfaction" and "customers' perception of value." This reinforces the two natural customer laws: 1) Customers go where they get good value, and 2) Customers go where they are treated well.

In the past, we would have said, "That's that," and gone on to some fluffy filler about a friendly smile in every aisle. Now we know better.

What you need as a small-business owner is a checklist of what customers really want. Then you can evaluate your business objectively to see how you compare with your competitors—big-box or independent.

As we listened to what customers told us about their service expectations, we discovered that *every* customer-service definition we received fit neatly into one of four categories. There is an interesting parallel here. Three decades ago, Dr. Phillip Kottler, academic marketing theory's foremost guru, shook up the marketing world by defining marketing by using the four P's.

Now we are going to forever change the way customer service is defined. Remember, you read it here first.

The Four P's of Service

Every customer definition, every customer expectation, and every element needed to help you turn onetime buyers into lifelong customers is contained in the four P's of service. What are these power P's? And how did we discover them?

The four P's are Place, People, Products, and Policies. We discovered them by accident.

We were trying to categorize the answers to our survey question, "What is customer service?" We found that some answers related to the human elements of service (People). Others had to do with store locations and facilities (Place). Still others were procedural (Policies), and a final category was needed for issues related to the actual merchandise being offered (Product). And just like that, the "Four P's of Service" were born.

Every business must deal with the four P's regardless of the type or industry. No business is exempt from them. Some will be better than others at one P or another. But every successful competitor will need to improve in all four areas.

As we discuss the individual "P's," and give examples based on our survey results, think about how well you deal with each customer-service issue. Highlight those areas where you know you need to make improvements. It's just that easy to create a checklist for customer-service improvement.

We are aware that there is some overlap on a few of these items. For example, "clean stores." Does that best fit in the "Place" P, the "Policies" P, or the "People" P? We tried to take each specific item to the root source. But if don't agree with where we've placed a customer's response, move it to where you feel it fits.

The First P—Place

In the usual context of retail and service business, the place is a location to which the customer must come. In some businesses, there are no "brick and mortar" locations, or the locations are not relevant to a customer's decision to do business with a particular company. For example, an Internet-based company may not have a "building" per se, and a plumber may work out of a low-rent warehouse accessible only from an alley. For the Internet company, the location is a digital domain, and for the plumber, the location is not important.

After all, you don't take your stopped-up drain to the plumber's shop to have it cleared.

In our survey, customers defined service as related to location—tangible and intangible—like this:

- Convenient locations (close to me)
- One-stop shopping
- Plenty of parking, close to the business
- Signs to tell me where things are
- Clean floors, shelves, and windows
- The exterior and parking lot are well-lit at night (safe)
- Clean, convenient restrooms
- No steps or stairs to negotiate
- Easy access from busy streets
- Handicap parking
- Well-lighted interior
- Wide aisles where two carts can pass
- Soft, pleasant background music
- A Web site that loads quickly
- Web sites that are easy to navigate

The Second P—People

For the sake of simplicity, we will narrow the definition of the 'people' factor to include only those individuals who have direct customer contact. We refer to these folks as front-line employees. We are aware that management plays a critical part in service success, and that no customer service effort can succeed without top-down support. However, we feel that management directly influences and controls overall policy rather than individual customer contact. (Read through the survey responses and see if you don't agree.)

Dot-com companies cannot ignore the people factor either. Each inquiry for information, product order, and order follow-up request comes from a person. (A customer or potential customer.) People prefer to do business with people. The popularity of ATM machines is an exception. And in our opinion, ATM machines would never have become necessary, if banks have been open more convenient hours.

In our survey, customers defined the "people" factors of service like this:

- Knowledgeable salespeople

- Help when I need it

- Being waited on by someone who is fun

- People with good attitudes

- Common courtesy

- Being greeted by someone who cares

- Someone who thanks me for my patronage

- Personal contact—being called by name

- People who smile—a lot

- A real person who answers the phone—not voice mail

- Carryout assistance

The Third P—Products

Company offerings are usually defined as "products or services." We want to be more inclusive in our consideration of the third P. In our minds—and for the purpose of this discussion—we are going to say that a service company provides a product.

While we will treat products and services as products, we do recognize one glaring difference. Products nearly always come from someplace far away and are made by people we don't know, while on the other hand, "service products" are usually local.

Therefore, product failure is seldom taken personally, while a "service product" is usually purchased from someone we know—or least have met or seen. When service breaks down, we do take it personally.

Evaluate the following survey responses carefully. See if you can pick out the areas where customers may have stronger personal feelings.

- They have what I want in stock.

- Several items to choose from.

- Getting exactly what I ordered.

- Quality products.

- Brand names I know and trust.

- Having special requests honored.

- Keeping promises.

- Products that deliver what they claim.

- Prices that give reasonable value.

The Fourth P—Policies

Customer-service policies are the guidelines and principles that govern how a business deals with its customers. These policies influence store operation, services provided, how employees are trained, and how customers are allowed to pay.

Customer service policy is typically a top-down system. Owners and managers usually establish the guidelines on how their stores will operate. They set store hours, choose payment methods, and decide how employees should be trained.

While this top-down system is common, we found that many of the successful competitors rely on the input of their front-line employees to find ways to improve service (bottom-up). In other words, the policies are not set in stone. A store policy is only used until someone comes up with a better policy idea.

The following responses to our customer survey should give you a starting point in evaluating your own customer-service policies.

- The store is open when I want to shop.

- Credit availability.

- They take personal checks.

- Being able to return things easily.

- Pay-at-the-pump gas stations.

- No waiting in long lines at the checkout.

Improving Your Service

Here's a seven-step plan for improving your customer service using the Four P's. Remember, your goal is to keep customers coming back. Building a lifetime relationship is the ultimate objective.

Step One—*Assume Your Service Is Bad.* Do not overestimate the strength of your customer service. Most small-business owners rate their service at a much higher level than their customers do.

Start with the assumption that your service is bad, or at least can be improved. Assume that your lack of service is causing customers to shop at other stores. It can't hurt, and it will get you started on looking for ways to improve.

Step Two—*Make a Service Checklist.* List the customer-service definitions from previous pages on four separate sheets of paper, using the basic headings of Place, People, Products, and Policies.

You can move any of the items from one category to another if you wish. It doesn't matter which sheet they are on, as long as you include them in your four-page checklist.

Step Three—*Do a Competitive Analysis.* You know who your most serious competitors are. Do an item-by-item analysis on your own, comparing your level of service in each area to your competitors'. Be as objective as you can in this step. Your goal is to identify several areas of weakness.

In the next step, you'll bring in your service team to help formulate a plan of attack. But first, you should do your own evaluation. Once you have identified areas where you are weak, prioritize those areas for action later.

Step Four—*Involve Your Service Team.* Anyone who has customer contact in your business should be involved in the process of improving your service. Find a meeting time that will fit everyone's schedule, and start with one of the P's. Go over the list of "what customers want" with your team.

Ask your team, "How can we improve in this area?" Don't ask team members how they think you're doing. You're not looking for their opinions. Work from the assumption that your service is bad and must be improved. What you want from your team is ideas for improvement.

Step Five—*Try for Triples.* Encourage your team members to come up with at least three suggestions for each item on the list. Use the brainstorming technique to achieve this. Do not evaluate or criticize suggestions; just write them down.

If the list goes to four, five, or six suggestions, that's great. You can always go back and cull the list or prioritize the suggestions and implement the best ideas first.

Step Six—*Create a Service-Improvement Plan.* Once you've gathered your team's suggestions for improving service, go back to the evaluation you conducted in Step Three. Select the top priority from each P list.

Make your four top priorities your first four-week action plan. Each week, single out one weakness to work on.

For example, let's assume that in your evaluation of the "Place" element you identified "store cleanliness" as your number one priority. The emphasis for week one would be "Keeping the store clean."

Next, list your team's suggestions and assign responsibilities. (This can be done on a single sheet that is posted and given to each employee.) Each day rotate the responsibilities so that each team member has responsibility for each suggestion.

For week two, select the next priority, print the suggestions and team member assignments, and be sure to include a reminder about the previous week's emphasis. You can use something like "Don't forget to keep the store clean."

If your competitive assessment shows twelve or fewer areas that need improvement, you can go to a monthly action plan. Use the same process as with the weekly action plan, but add new emphasis areas on a monthly basis.

Step Seven—*Reevaluate.* After a few months, go back and review your original competitive analysis from Step Three. Note areas where you've made progress and where you still need improvement.

Improving your customer service is not a onetime campaign. It is an ongoing process of moving from one level of service to a higher level. Those companies who continually raise the bar will be the most successful at keeping customers for life.

When You Blow It

We all love to get compliments on how well we're doing in business. Mark Twain said he could work a month on one good compliment. Without a doubt, having a customer brag about our service endears us to that person.

But what about that person who is not happy and makes it a point to tell you about it? What about the person who complains about your products or service? Do you feel friendly toward them?

If you truly care about keeping customers for life, you should realize that a person who is displeased and takes time to let you know is truly a friend to your business. When someone points out a service problem, they give you a chance to improve. When a customer complains that you've blown it, they give you an opportunity to distinguish your business from the masses who do nothing when a customer is unhappy.

The customer who is hardest on a business is the "silent, but deadly" customer. Retailing guru Marshall Field said, "Only those hurt me who are displeased but do not complain. They refuse me permission to correct my errors and thus improve my service."

Consider the following statistics:

- For every customer who bothers to complain, there are more than twenty others who will remain silent.

- The average "wronged" customer will tell fifteen other people.

- Nine of ten unhappy customers will never buy from you again.

Fortunately, a single service problem is unlikely to completely destroy the customer's confidence in your business. (Assuming you resolve the problem effectively.) There are a few instances where one mistake is all you get. Examples would include:

- *Dishonesty.* Such as changing a contract after the customer has signed it, or lying to a customer, or substituting an inferior product.

- *Lewd Behavior or Sexual Harassment.* No explanation needed.

- *Any Illegal Activity.* Such as an accountant who would try to resolve a taxpayer's complaint regarding taxes owed by suggesting claiming false deductions.

Smart companies encourage feedback from customers and even solicit it. What happens in your company when a customer has a problem? In terms of generating repeat business, what happens *after* the sale is as important as what happens *before* the sale.

Unfortunately, it doesn't take much to ruin a business relationship that may have taken a great deal of time, effort, and money to build. You may have a beautiful store, great displays, and quality merchandise, but if you don't consistently treat your customers well, they will beat a path to your competitors' doors.

Two of the biggest sources of customer complaints are rude and indifferent service, and promises that aren't delivered. Even in a business that strives to provide customers with excellent service, there will always be people who have complaints.

When a customer approaches you with a complaint, you really have two issues with which to deal: working through the customer's emotions and resolving the complaint. Remember this: When the customer believes there's a problem, you have a problem.

When someone has a complaint, remember to *keep your cool.* When someone is angry, it's easy to get defensive, but it only makes matters worse. The person with the cool head will control the situation.

Create a Customer-Recovery Plan

Having a specific plan of action for resolving problems will not only help your business in resolving complaints, but also help you recover that customer for life.

Early work done by customer-recovery experts Ron Zemke and Chip Bell shows what customers expect when they bring problems to the attention of a business. Their research indicates five main expectations:

1. To receive a sincere apology

2. To be offered a *fair solution* for the problem

3. To be treated in a way that shows the company cares about the problem and helping the customer solve it

4. To be offered a solution that is equivalent to the burden the customer has endured

5. To receive the complete solution and not have the results fall short

Keep these expectations in mind as you use the *ALERT* customer-recovery method.

A = *Acknowledge the problem and apologize.* By admitting that there is a problem, you begin to diffuse the angry or upset customer. By apologizing, you make them feel that they have some power in finding a solution. Introduce yourself, and get the customer's name and address if you can.

L = *Listen to the answers after you invite them to tell you what happened.* You cannot solve a problem you don't fully understand. Allow them to vent some steam, if they need to. By listening carefully, you show the customer you're concerned. Don't interrupt what they are saying, but offer empathetic phrases like "I see what you mean" or "I understand."

E = *Engage in a fact-finding dialogue.* Once the customer has vented some steam, ask open-ended questions that will help you get the facts while the customer does most of the talking. What happened? What should have happened? How did it happen? What does the customer want to happen now? Remember, your purpose is to gather information, not assess blame or find fault. You can work on correcting the problem internally after the unhappy customer is happy again and has left your business.

R = *Repeat the problem as you understand it and record the information.* Take notes and verify facts. Unfortunately, not all problems can be resolved on the spot, so you may need the information in the future. Taking good notes shows your commitment to finding a solution and will serve as a long-standing record.

T = *Thank the customer for telling you about it and take action.* As difficult as it is to take criticism, the only way to solve a problem is to know about it. You want to create an atmosphere where customers know that you want to hear from them if their needs aren't satisfied.

Ask the customer to propose a solution. Ask, "What would you like for us to do?" or the ultimate disarmer, "What do you think is fair?" If the request is realistic, do it. If not, explain what you can do. If the customer doesn't know what he or she wants, suggest some options. Once you agree on the best solution, take action, and follow up. Thank the customer again for advising you of the problem and for his or her understanding.

Keep in mind that the most important ingredient in the problem-solving process is courtesy. Your attitude should convey genuine concern and consideration. Stay friendly and pleasant. Don't interrupt, and don't correct. It doesn't really matter how right you are if you lose a customer who may tell twenty or more people about the experience.

Bad luck for you if that dissatisfied customer happens to be a writer for a national publication. When that happens—and it has—the "unsatisfied customer" won't just tell twenty other people, but 2 million or more. Maybe we should treat each customer as if they could possibly write a damaging article . . . or produce an expose on national television.

And for a final note, remember what your mother told you, "You can't please everybody." Unlike some experts, we don't believe the adage that "the customer is always right." No one, for instance, has the right to be rude or abusive to you or your employees. If that happens, evaluate your options, consider an offer to refund their money, and give them a subtle invitation to take their business elsewhere.

Keep Getting Feedback

Every time you get feedback from a customer, it gives you an opportunity to improve something about your business. The most successful companies we know are diligent about monitoring customer opinions. Choose methods that best suit your needs and budget, but make your effort to solicit customer opinions an *ongoing* one.

Here are a few ideas:

- *Customer Visits.* As you walk through your store, ask your customers, "How are we doing?" Encourage feedback.

- *Customer Surveys.* Design simple, easy-to-read surveys and post them in a prominent location. Invite customers to fill them out and drop them in a box in your store or use a postage-paid card. (We give you some examples in Chapter Nine.)

- *Focus Groups.* Invite a small group of people—usually five to eight people, no more than ten—to come to your store and share their opinions and suggestions about your business. The session might last an hour or two and should be led by a professional who is skilled in communications and getting people to give honest opinions. Provide refreshments and give each participant a thank-you gift, such as a gift certificate, for participating. It's best to videotape or record the meeting. Listen carefully to what your customers are saying, and don't become defensive.

- *Employee Surveys.* The ones who know your customers best are your employees, and they hear firsthand the comments being made. Establish a system for employees to note customer opinions, but do this in conjunction with other programs, since some may not reveal criticisms of management or their own work.

Ten Loyalty Builders

Here are ten simple things that every business can do to ensure that your customers will remain your customers. Use them to build loyalty, increase sales, and ensure quality referrals.

1. *Hire good employees, train them well, and treat them fairly.* (We have devoted all of Chapter Five to finding, motivating, and keeping quality employees.) Remember, to your customers, your employees are your business.

2. *Keep employees informed.* Customers find it irritating when employees aren't aware of special sales, promotions, or inventory. Keeping everyone in the loop makes for happy customers and employees.

3. *Make customer service everyone's job.* Providing good service is the only way your employees can improve the quality of their job. Their pay, benefits, and job satisfaction all depend on how well they serve the customer. It is everyone's job to see that every

customer is delighted every time. No one in any organization should ever use the phrase "It's not my job."

4. *Keep your promises and keep your word.* One of the best ways to build trust and loyalty is to do what you said you would do. In Chapter Six, you'll learn the value of going beyond keeping your word.

   There's a Russian proverb that says, "Don't put it in my ear, but in my hand." Promises may win the customer once, but performance will keep them coming back.

5. *Learn your customer's name, and use it.* A wise person once said that there was no sound sweeter in any language than one's own name. If you want to win customers and make them feel special, call them by name. Even the clerks at the megastores are sharp enough to look at checks and credit cards and use the customer's name.

6. *Value your customer's time.* No one has the time or patience to stand in long lines to check out or return merchandise. You prove that you value your customers when you show them that you value their time. Time is a semi-precious commodity, so let your customers keep as much of it as you can.

7. *Find something to do every day that surprises, excites, or delights a customer.* Everyone like surprises as long as they are good surprises. We know a family who went to a famous theme park on a special discount vacation package. When they arrived at their hotel, there was no reservation in the computer and no accommodation like the one they had reserved available. Surprise! The family wasn't turned away; instead, the hotel upgraded them to a two-bedroom suite at no additional cost. Surprised! Excited! Delighted! Loyal!

8. *Empower your people to solve problems.* In the above example, the hotel manager was away. The clerk at the front desk had the authority to solve the problem. Hire the right people, train them well, and give them both the responsibility and authority to take care of your customers' needs.

9. *Say thanks to your customers.* Not only is saying "Thank you" good manners, it is also good business. One merchant we know looks through the checks and credit card receipts every day. Every purchase over a predetermined amount gets a handwritten thank-you note. Some days, it may be one or two, others as many as a dozen. She considers writing the thank-you notes time well spent.

10. *Constantly monitor your service success.* Ask your customers how you're doing. Find out what they think. Listen carefully and respond to their answers. Some businesses hire mystery shoppers, others ask customers directly, and some use surveys. Have your employees listen for customer observations and comments. Remember, you can't fix problems that you aren't aware of.

Keep Them Coming Back

Good service is the best form of marketing we know of. If you follow the Four P's and do a great job in each area, your reward will be happy customers who will be loyal for life. Word-of-mouth referrals—marketing—will help you generate business without spending a dime on promotion.

Each encounter with a prospective customer or an existing one is an opportunity to acquire a lifelong fan. As Stanley Marcus, the father of retail, said, "Nobody owns anybody anymore." All business is competitive business, folks, and you're only as good as your last performance. Strive to satisfy *every* customer, *every* time, and they will keep coming back for encores, and you'll be assured of many repeat opportunities.

Key Points Checklist

☑ Never lose sight of the only reason your business exists . . . to serve the customer.

☑ The customer always defines service.

☑ There are four areas where every business must ensure that service is top-notch.

☑ These areas are: 1. *Place*—your business location; 2. *People*—your employees who have customer contact; 3. *Products*—the quality you sell; and 4. *Policies*—the guidelines you establish for how your customers will be treated.

☑ When the customer believes there's a problem, you have a problem.

☑ Successful competitors get continual feedback on how they are doing.

Service Is an Attitude CHAPTER 5

First-rate people hire first-rate people; second-rate people hire third-rate people.

—LEO ROSTEN

You become what you hire. We have never seen a business outperform the quality of the people it hires. Most small-business owners tell us that one of their biggest management headaches is finding, hiring, and keeping good people.

Ironically, the people who do most of the hiring for a small business usually lack the skills and experience to do a good job. Business owners are seldom trained in personnel issues. All too often they make hasty decisions based on how they "feel" about a candidate after the briefest of interviews.

Our goal in this chapter is to help you improve your ability to make intelligent hiring decisions so that you choose the person that is best suited for the job you are trying to fill. We will do this by helping you understand the hiring process, and by sharing concepts, techniques, and methods that will allow you to enhance your odds of hiring success.

One of the best ways to set your business apart from the megastores is to give your customers personal attention and services that only quality people can provide. Remember that in Chapter Four we stressed the importance of building lifetime relationships with your customers. Great people are more likely to build lasting relationships because they understand the value of taking good care of their customers.

Common Hiring Mistakes

The first element in improving your hiring skills is to know some of the most common hiring mistakes. Here are six errors that are often made by inexperienced managers.

1. *Not Analyzing the Job Thoroughly.* The result of this error is that you may not fully understand the skills, experience, and education needed to do the job well.

2. *Not Advertising the Job Effectively.* This mistake often cuts down on the number of qualified applicants.

3. *Not Starting the Search Early Enough.* When you are under time pressure, you are much more likely to hire the wrong person.

4. *Not Conducting Thorough Interviews.* Hasty interviews often lead to insufficient information on which to base a hiring decision.

5. *Not Being Diligent in Checking References.* One business owner told us he never checks references because he knows they will only say good things about the person who used them as a reference. One of the best pieces of advice we've ever received on this topic is to check references that aren't given. It takes a little extra effort, but you can learn a lot.

6. *Relying on a "Gut Feeling."* Feelings will never take the place of facts. If your only hiring justification is a feeling, you don't have enough facts.

The Hiring Process

Webster's defines "process" as "a particular method of doing something, generally involving a number of steps or operations." The hiring process we are going to share with you has been proven by successful business owners. It contains ten steps that will guide you through the hiring maze, and will help you avoid the common mistakes.

Step One: *Create a Place Where People Want to Work.* If you have a good reputation for paying well, treating people right, and nurturing employees, it will be much easier to find people to hire. In step two, we'll show you what employees are looking for in a workplace.

We recommend that you study the factors in step two, and then evaluate how your business stacks up. Be objective. Everyone has some built-in biases, but the more honest you are, the better the process works. Do you regularly provide the things that most employees want? If you have some weak areas, we would suggest that you address those issues before you get too far in the hiring process.

Make a brief list of the main factors and see how many you offer your employees. We are finding that benefits and job flexibility are increasingly important to younger workers.

Step Two: *Know What Employees Want.* Every business has a reputation in the community. Yours is either known as a good place to work or a bad place. You can improve your reputation and your ability to attract quality people by providing what employees want. Here is an up-to-date list of what employees are looking for in the workplace.

- *Good Health Insurance and Benefits.* The rising costs of health care, prescriptions, and insurance are causing quality employees to reassess their priorities. They will often accept lower salaries if a solid benefits package is offered.

- *Interesting Work.* While the definition of "interesting" varies from person to person, nearly all employees are looking for new challenges, variety, and responsibility.

- *Fair Wages.* Great employees will do an honest day's work for you if you treat them right and pay them fairly. It's very difficult to expect loyalty, enthusiasm, and commitment when you're paying less than the going rate. The successful businesses we interviewed typically pay *above* the industry average for similar jobs.

- *To Be Included in the Decision-Making Process.* Great employees want opportunities to offer input in discussions that affect them and their jobs.

- *A Caring Environment.* In the intense struggle to survive against the mass merchandisers and supercompetition, it may seem superficial to say that the way to get more out of employees is to truly care about them. But think about it. Who would you work harder for? The boss who really cares about you or the one who believes you're only a ticket to the bottom line?

- *A Job that's Fun.* Even in the most demanding jobs, don't overlook the importance of having some fun. It's not inconsistent with operating a serious, profit-making business. Companies that have more fun get more done.

- *To Feel Valued for the Work They Accomplish.* Recognition is one of the easiest, and most important, motivators. Catch your employees doing something right and praise them for a *specific* behavior or results.

- *A Job that's Satisfying and Significant.* You will hire and retain better employees if they enjoy their work. And if the workplace is enjoyable, you'll find that absenteeism dips as well as claims for disabilities related to job stress.

Step Three: *Know What You Need.* A common problem in the hiring process is mismatching people and positions. This often leads to unhappiness between both parties and usually causes an employee to look for other opportunities. You can eliminate most of this problem by creating *clear, concise job descriptions*.

A good job description will define the responsibilities and requirements of the job. In addition, it should be used to assign levels of importance to all job functions. You may wish to start by listing all duties and responsibilities the job requires. Then go back over the list and assign each item an importance level. This can be as simple as: very important, important, or not too important.

At the end of this section, we have included "Hiring Tools." Two of the tools we have included are sample job descriptions. The first is a simple one detailing the position of "retail sales clerk." The second one is more complex because the job it describes is a higher-level position with more functions and responsibilities.

Step Four: *Start Early.* If you have at least one employee, you are going to be surprised one day when someone you believed was a "happy camper" gives you his or her two-week notice. If you have not anticipated future vacancies, you may find yourself in a real time crunch to fill the spot.

Unfortunately when situations like this occur, you may discover one of the truisms of hiring: The more urgent your need, the more likely you are to hire the wrong person. You can avoid this situation by beginning the search for good employees before you actually need them. The successful companies we've studied take a proactive approach to hiring rather than reacting to a vacancy when it occurs. In essence, they recruit all the time. You can too.

Have you ever been impressed by an employee in a restaurant, store, bank, or other business and thought, "Boy, I'd love to have him working for me?" When that happens, don't just conclude your business and leave. Introduce yourself, and tell him how he has impressed you. Keep a list of candidates for future reference.

Explain that you periodically have openings in your business and would like to keep his name on file. The worst that can happen is that he'll be flattered to know his good work has impressed someone—but isn't interested in changing jobs. The best thing is that you'll begin a resource file of people who may fit in well with your company.

We know a specialty store chain whose managers have cards saying, "I was impressed by your service. If you're ever looking for a job, please call me."

We believe that good hiring is an ongoing process. When you invest time and effort in the process, you will find that the rewards outweigh the effort.

Step Five: *Know Where to Look.* Where are the best people? They are working for good companies, good organizations, and good families. Therefore, placing an ad in the classifieds may not reach the most qualified candidates. They are already working and most likely are only casually looking at the "help wanted" ads, if at all.

Here are some tips for finding the best people:

1. *Develop a Referral Network.* It's easier to analyze a few good prospects who come highly recommended by people you trust than to search for a pearl from a stack of applications and resumes. Your network should include your most trusted employees, customers with whom you have built a long-term relationship, suppliers and vendors that you know well, and respected business friends.

2. *Consult Local Placement Offices, Colleges, and Technical Schools.* Depending on the job requirements, these can be excellent sources of finding people who meet your job criteria. You will want to have copies of your job description to e-mail or fax to your contacts. This helps ensure that the specific requirements are understood.

3. *Advertise the Position.* As you develop your advertising, keep in mind that you are "selling" the job and the company to prospective employees. Make the ads brief, but make the job and the company sound exciting and interesting. List qualifications, but avoid using terms such as "boy," "youthful," "girl Friday," or other potentially discriminatory terms.

4. *Retain an Employment Agency or Headhunter.* Though there will be expenses involved, agencies can do some of the initial screening for you, which may save time and money in the long run.

5. *Post the Job with Your State Employment Commission.* This is usually more effective for entry-level and low-skills jobs, but one never knows when a pearl may show up among the oysters.

6. *Attend Job Fairs*. Many communities have annual job fairs where potential employees can meet with employers. The advantage of these events is that you may meet several good prospects in a short period of time.

Step Six: *Know What to Look For.* Quality people have some common traits. In Chapter Two we detailed ten traits of great employees. They are: high self-esteem, good communication skills, self-motivation, dependability, energy and dedication to hard work, a positive attitude, perseverance, enthusiasm, a sense of humor, and integrity.

While some of these characteristics may be more important to certain jobs, all of them are desirable for most positions. If we can't have them all, we'll start with a positive attitude and integrity. Our experience has taught us not to hire anyone who doesn't have these two qualities.

Step Seven: *Sell the Job and Your Company.* Quality people want to work for quality companies. As a small-business owner you have some unique advantages to offer prospects. For example, you can know every employee personally, you can act as a *coach* and *mentor*, you can inspire feelings of individual responsibility, you can individualize personal growth and career potential, you can inspire creativity and initiative, you can help new employees establish good relationships with customers, and you can offer flexibility that larger firms will not.

These advantages must be sold. Potential employees must be told what you offer in addition to salary, benefits, and so on. While you shouldn't exaggerate or oversell the job or your company, it is in your best interest to extol the positives of the job and the firm.

Step Eight: *Hire Tough.* It is better to hire no one than to hire the wrong one. Here are some tips on hiring tough.

First, create an application form for all interested parties to complete as a first step toward employment. The application should capture previous employment data, starting and ending dates for all jobs, immediate supervisors' names, educational information, personal data (address, phone numbers, and references), and the applicant's interests and hobbies.

We prefer to have the application filled out in our presence. You would be amazed at the differences we uncover when the application and the resume are filled out at separate times.

Second, compare the application and the resume and note any differences. Prepare questions to discover why the differences occurred.

Third, ask for character and work-related references. We believe it is smart to talk to all references even though we expect them to be biased in a positive manner. We also believe in digging out references that were not furnished. It takes very little effort to find others who worked with the applicant or were friends or neighbors.

Fourth, conduct thorough, in-depth interviews with the most qualified candidates. (See Step Nine for methods of creating a solid interview plan.)

Step Nine: *Create an Interview Plan.* The goals of the interview are to find out what the candidate has done, why he or she did it, and how well it was done. In addition, we want to determine if the candidate can do the job, is willing to do the job, and is manageable and would fit in with the rest of your team.

It is impossible to achieve the above goals if you go into the interview unprepared. You will never get the results you want if you "wing it" when you interview.

Begin the interview process by outlining the interview and how you want it to go. Then prepare a list of questions to ask. Good interviewers let the candidate do most of the talking. As a rule of thumb the candidate should be talking 75 to 80 percent of the time. Force yourself to become a better listener.

The next step is to narrow the field to a smaller group of finalists, and set them up for multiple interviews. We would suggest that you schedule the interviews for different times of the day. Once again have a list of prepared questions ready. One successful owner who conducts multiple interviews always holds one of the interviews during a meal. She often disqualifies candidates who talk with their mouths full, chew with their mouths open, and in general exhibit bad table manners.

We recommend that you take careful notes during the interview, and that you fill out your evaluation form immediately after the interview. We also think it's wise to have a key employee join you for the interviews. Let them focus on the note-taking and see if their observations match yours.

At the end of this section, we have provided a sample interview plan, a list of good interview questions, and a sample evaluation form. Please feel free to copy and/or modify any of these items for your personal use.

Step Ten: *Get Your New Hire off to a Fast Start.* You went through the hiring process, found the perfect candidate, welcomed them aboard, and then left them to fend for themselves.

Bad idea. The first week may be the most important forty hours you ever spend with your new hire. All employees are a little anxious about their first day. Here are some suggestions for getting new folks up to speed.

1. *Make them feel at home.* Rather than focusing on the importance of the job, concentrate on putting them at ease. The first day should include introductions, a tour of the facilities, company policies and rules, and who to call in case of emergencies.

    Take care of necessary forms and paperwork. Review the company's mission and annual goals. Detail pay periods, hours, breaks, and safety information. Give the employee plenty of time and opportunity for questions.

2. *Don't expect too much too soon.* You may need your new employee to be productive right now, but in reality that seldom happens. Give them time to adjust to their new environment and routine. You and other key employees can set the tone of what is expected.

3. *Give your new hire good directions.* The most frustrating time for new employees may be that period when they don't exactly

know what to do. Without proper guidance they may do the wrong thing, or they may do the right thing in the wrong way. Clearly define your expectations and the results you want. If possible, assign a buddy or mentor to the new employee.

4. *Add responsibilities gradually.* Your goal is to allow each employee to grow and assume responsibility as quickly as possible. There is a fine line here. You do not want to overwhelm them, but you don't want to bore your quick studies either. Add new tasks and responsibilities gradually, and monitor their progress.

5. *Stay in close contact.* Show your new hires that you are interested in their progress. Give them opportunities to ask questions and seek your approval. By staying in close contact you can nip problems in the bud. You can also correct negative behavior before it becomes a bad habit.

When you use this hiring process and the tools we've included, you will hire a more productive and motivated workforce. You will lower employee turnover, cut absenteeism, and get fewer customer complaints.

Hiring Tools

We have created some simple tools to use during the hiring process. Please feel free to modify these tools to fit your needs and job requirements.

Sample Job Descriptions

POSITION: Retail Sales Clerk

GENERAL DUTIES: Responsibilities include: Serving customers, ringing up customer purchases, answering the phone, keeping the display areas attractive, stocking merchandise, light cleaning—dusting, vacuuming—and other duties as assigned.

HOURS: (32–40 hours/week) Some weekend work is required.

REPORTS TO: Assistant manager and store owner

EXPERIENCE AND SKILLS REQUIRED: Position requires an outgoing person who enjoys working with people, with good communication skills, excellent manners, knowledge of ranch products, and a clean-cut appearance. Previous retail experience considered a plus.

SALARY RANGE: $6.75 to $8.00 per hour to start.

LOCATION: Murphy's Feed Mart, 610 Main Street, Sage, Nebraska

POSITION: Vice-President and Chief Financial Officer

GENERAL DUTIES: Primary responsibilities include: Preparation of all financial reports, design of computer software system to incorporate records of five store locations into one combined set of financial statements, implementation of new barcode software system, coordinating all financial operations with auditors. Secondary responsibilities include: Providing weekly owner reports on inventory levels, dated accounts receivable schedule, dated accounts payable schedule, and individual store reports for all five stores. The CFO will provide monthly reports and analysis at the store manager's meetings.

REPORTS TO: Store owner

EXPERIENCE, EDUCATION, AND SKILLS REQUIRED: Master's degree in accounting or financial management required, CPA preferred, at least five years' experience at CFO level.

SALARY AND BENEFITS: Salary: Commensurate with experience. Benefits: Paid health insurance, two weeks' vacation the first year, dental plan, and car allowance.

LOCATION: Bill's House of Music, 411 Elm Street, Canyon, Kentucky

Sample Interviewer's Evaluation Form

Position: _____

Candidate's Name: _____

Date: _____

Interviewer: _____

QUALIFICATIONS	RATING				
	EXCELLENT	**ABOVE AVERAGE**	**SATISFACTORY**	**SOME DEFICIENCIES**	**UNACCEPTABLE**
Experience					
Attitude					
Communication Skills					
Appearance					
Personality					
Special Skills					
Dependable					
Motivated					

Comments: _____

_____

_____

Strengths: _____

_____

_____

Weaknesses: _____

_____

_____

The Four Phases of the Interview Plan

Part One: (5 to 10 minutes) *The Get Acquainted Phase.* The objective in this part of the interview is to put the candidate at ease. This is the time to describe the job as you see it, and give a little history on the business. It is also a good time to clarify any questions about the candidate's application or resume.

Part Two: (30 to 40 minutes) *The Questioning Phase.* In this part, you begin to plumb the depths of the candidate's experience, skills, motivation, and personality. Remember, your goal is to find out what the candidate has done, how well he or she did it, and what his or her motivation was for doing it. In part two, you should ask open-ended questions, and then follow them up, request clarification, and listen carefully.

You should let the candidate talk 75 to 80 percent of the time. Your job is to ask a question, listen carefully, and take good notes. We prefer to interview with an associate present to take notes and give us feedback.

Part Three: (5 to 10 minutes) *The Summary and Closing Phase.* Thank the candidate and let him or her know that you appreciate his or her interest. Ask if they have any questions or final thoughts. If not, thank him or her again and advise him or her that you will let him or her know the outcome in a few days, or better yet by a specific date.

Part Four: *The Evaluation Phase.* We recommend completing the evaluation form immediately after the interview. Don't wait to evaluate all candidates at one time. After some time passes, all candidates will begin to blur together. Score each candidate and record your perceptions while they are fresh on your mind.

Great Interview Questions

Starter Questions: If we were going to make a hiring decision solely on what you tell us about yourself, what would you want us to know?

If we talked to people who knew you well, what words would they use to describe you?

Attitude:

Have you ever lost in competition? How did you feel?

Do you feel like you've made a success of life to date? How?

Who was your best boss? Describe the person.

What duties did you like most in your job? Least?

How do you feel about working with other employees?

Motivation:

How did you prepare for this interview?

Why did you leave your last job?

What obstacles have you overcome to get where you are today?

What have you done on your own to prepare for a better job?

Initiative:

Do you prefer to work alone or with others?

What do you like and dislike about your last job?

When have you felt like giving up on a task?

Stability:

How do you get along with people you dislike?

What do you most admire in others?

What things do some people do that are irritating to you?

What were your most unpleasant work experiences?

Planning:

How do you spend a typical day?

Where do you want to be five years from now?

What part of your work do you like best?

What part is the most difficult for you?

Insight:

What are your strengths and weaknesses?

What are you doing to change your weaknesses into strengths?

How did you react to criticism in your last job?

Social Skills:	What do you like to do in your spare time?
	What kind of people do you get along with best?
	Do you prefer making new friends or keeping old ones?
Last Question:	Why should we hire you?

Grow with Training

You've accomplished the first step by finding and hiring the right employees. The next crucial step is training them. While many small companies make the effort to find and hire good people, few will invest much time or money in training. Then they wonder why employees don't measure up to expectations.

It's like investing the time and effort to select and plant a beautiful rose bush, then depriving it of water, fertilizer, and sunlight. You'll likely get thorns, but not very many roses in full, glorious bloom.

Training is an ongoing process. Just as the rose needs constant nutrients, your employees will grow into better, more productive employees if they are constantly nurtured, evaluated, and trained.

Chip Averwater, owner of Amro Music Stores, Inc. in Memphis, has some great ideas to share in the area of training. Averwater says, "Training and education isn't a frill at Amro—it's a vital ingredient in our success."

Averwater has the following tools for his employees to use to learn and grow personally:

- A company library well-stocked with books, videos, and audio-tapes.

- Training manuals covering personnel issues, salesmanship, and product information.

- Testing materials on each of the manuals the employees receive. Each employee is required to take and pass a test on each manual prior to qualifying for commission on what they sell.

- Each new employee is matched with an experienced salesperson for one-to-one coaching.

- Every quarter the company holds a half-day sales training meeting.

Averwater sums up his success in this area like this. "The training takes time, but it is popular with our people. They recognize the value of increasing their skills and value. They have pride in their expertise and enjoy serving their customers."

Resources for Training

In any training program, it's important to start with a clear idea of what you expect your employees to learn. Is it to upgrade job skills, learn new techniques, or just become more motivated? Set specific objectives for training.

First-class training programs don't have to cost a lot of money, but they do require some creative approaches. Here are some low-cost resources you can use to get started:

- *Other employees.* On-the-job training is the most widely used method of training. Your best trainers may be among your current employees.

- *Books, audiotapes, videos, and professional journals.* Start a training library and encourage employees to spend time there or give them specific assignments. You might develop a simple form for employees to use that asks them to describe what they have learned.

- *Seminars.* Available in a wide-variety of cost and quality, many seminar companies and professional speakers offer expertise on a wide range of topics. The important thing to remember here is to be sure employees share their knowledge with others and you're open to integrating new suggestions they've learned. Schedule mini–training sessions during lunch hours or in the first or last hour of the day.

- *Schools and colleges.* There is a wealth of knowledge available at local institutions of learning. Call local colleges, universities, or technical schools and inquire about experts in the field of choice. Community colleges in particular strive to build partnerships with businesses and may have training programs already in place. Small Business Development Centers offer regular small-business programs.

- *Consider asking employees to share in the costs of the training.* Many employers pay for training if employees pass the course or class. Some employers require their employees to pay for the training if they fail. It's an incentive that works!

- *Your local chamber of commerce may also have the names of qualified speakers or trainers.* If not, they should be able to provide you with the names of people who might have those names.

- *Pool resources.* Contact other business owners who might benefit from the same type of training you think you and your employees need. Hire a good speaker or consultant or schedule a workshop and share the expenses with other companies.

Motivating a Winning Team

What would you give to have your employees arrive at work happy, enthusiastic, and ready to give their best at their jobs all day long? Surprisingly, it may be easier—and less expensive—than you might think.

Nine tips for motivating your employees:

1. *Give your employees the tools and resources to get their jobs done effectively.* Nothing can be so frustrating and defeating as making an employee struggle with equipment that is outmoded and ineffective. Investing money in equipment to help your employees get the job done efficiently is always a good investment—as long as they have the proper training to utilize it.

   Barry Steinberg, owner of Direct Tire and Auto Service, invests heavily in tools and technology to keep his employees productive and his customers happy. "Last year we spent $85,000 on new tire equipment, auto repair tools, and diagnostic electronics," Steinberg said. "We strive to be the best, and the equipment and training help us reach our quality goals.

2. *Constantly tell your employees how important they are, and show it in small and large ways.* Aledia Hunt Tush, who owns Mr. CB's, a marine sporting goods store in Sarasota, Florida, fully understands how important her employees are to the success of her business. "I will never take credit for this store by myself," she said. "My employees are extremely important, and anyone in business who doesn't understand that had better go back to school." How does she communicate that to her employees? "I tell them all the time," she said.

3. *Celebrate the special days in the lives of your employees.* Birthdays top the list, but employment anniversaries are important dates to remember, too. Whether you give your employee a holiday on their special day or a card or small gift, the message you send to them is, "You're important enough for me to remember your special days."

4. *"Praise publicly and criticize privately,"* as the adage goes. Catch your employees doing something right and praise them—publicly! If you must criticize, stay focused on the actions or behavior you object to. Tell them briefly, but specifically, what changes you want. And do it privately.

5. *Be sensitive to the family and personal responsibilities of your employees.* Companies that build loyalty and commitment have made tremendous strides toward helping employees deal with the delicate balancing act between work and personal life. Some offer flexible schedules; others offer job sharing. The common denominator is understanding and cooperation. The reward is employees who lead balanced, fulfilling lives, and who are willing to give 100 percent to their jobs.

Debbi Kramer, owner of Kari Lynn's Formal and Bridal Boutique, knows that flexibility is one of her strengths in employing several part-time people. Kramer says, "I tell new employees coming in that there are no big salaries here. What we offer is a fun place to work with flexible hours. We have several working moms, and we realize they need time off to take kids to the doctor, attend special events at schools, and have some balance in their lives. It works! I have great employees."

6. *Match the person to the job.* It's become clear over the years that the old adage that "anybody can do anything if they really put their minds to it" is simply not true. People who work in a job they're not well-suited for because of knowledge, temperament, or lack of training will be prone to stress and poor job performance. We're not saying that employees can *always* avoid jobs they don't like, but you'll get amazing results if you pair the person to the position.

Chip Averwater of Amro Music, Inc., hires only the best and only those applicants who are well-suited for the job. Averwater says, "We hire carefully, pay well, train thoroughly, and encourage growth and leadership. We do use a personality profile on every serious applicant so we know what jobs a candidate is best suited for. The profiles, which we refer to as 'surveys,' really help us match the person to the job."

7. *Keep the lines of communication open.* Keep employees informed and convey to them the role they play in your company's success. Hold informative meetings, even if they're casual.

8. *Set doable goals and encourage competition between your departments or teams.* Contests can spur energy and enthusiasm. Post the results daily. Recognize the winners, but be sure to encourage and congratulate the teams that don't win, too.

Jerrold Taylor of Monet DeSauw is a believer in the goal-setting process: "We've found that goals help us develop focus. Focus helps us produce the results we need. So results are the end products of the goals we set. In our business, every employee is a team member, and we all need to stay focused on our goals."

9. *If you don't have a bonus or profit-sharing plan, think about starting one.* Employees who have a stake in the success of their company will work harder to ensure its success.

Bill Hanson, Jr., owner of Reliable Office Systems, Inc., shares his thoughts on keeping folks motivated: "We start by paying competitive, fair wages. We set up incentive plans to help us retain key employees. Sometimes you have to pay a premium to work with the best."

The costs of these plans will likely be outweighed by the increase in employee loyalty and motivation. Take into account the high costs of continually advertising for, interviewing, and training new employees and the even-higher costs of poorly motivated employees.

When It Isn't Working: How to Fire Fairly

Change is a fact of life in every business, and it's important to accept the fact that no matter how hard you try and how carefully you plan, your business won't always be a great place to work for everyone you hire.

In a small business with few employees, the decision to fire someone can send ripples throughout the entire organization. How do you know when it's time to fire? You use the MOP Test to determine if your employee's actions are putting you and your company in jeopardy.

M = *Morale*. Is the problem employee having a negative influence on the morale and attitude of others?

O = *Operations*. Is the problem employee affecting operations, causing a decrease in productivity or increases in costs?

P = *Profits*. Are profits dropping because of the employee's actions? Are you losing customers, sales, or orders? All of these will eventually lead to a profit decline.

If you answered "yes," and if you can't change the employee's behavior, it may be time to fire him or her. If you elect to fire an employee, know your legal responsibilities.

Maybe you have a less-than-ideal employee who you believe holds some promise. To salvage this employee, consider the "Progressive Discipline" method.

Step One. *Counsel the employee, addressing behavior that is unacceptable.* Tactfully point out improper actions or behaviors, and suggest some steps for improving them. Be positive and encouraging, praising all strengths, but stress that the undesirable behavior must be stopped.

Many times, this first step is the only one that you will have to take. Good employees will often work hard at changing unsatisfactory behavior once they're aware of what they're doing wrong. Be sure to make notes of your discussion. Date and write the details of the conversation. If you don't see any improvement, go to the next step.

Step Two. *Written reprimand.* After the verbal counseling session, if the results are still not satisfactory, put the problem in writing. Clearly state deficiencies or improper behavior and review the verbal discussion. Issue written guidelines, with a timetable, to correct the behavior. Date your notes and get the employee's signature. It's still possible to salvage the employee at this point, but the chances are growing slimmer.

Step Three. *Final warning.* Make this blunt and to the point. Restate your previous discussions and written reprimand. Stress that this is the last chance for improvement. Point out that failure to meet your demands will result in termination. Detail your demands in writing, ask the employee to sign it, and put a copy in his or her personnel file.

If you still haven't seen improvement, fire quickly, and don't let the situation drag on. Remember that your employee has rights and feelings. Here are some suggestions:

- Never fire without being ready. Have the employee's final paycheck ready on the day you fire, including back pay, earned vacation, and severance pay, if applicable. If you provide insurance benefits, the employee has a right to keep them in effect, and you must tell them that.

- Don't fire in anger.
- Expect the worst, including anger, tears, verbal abuse, and more.
- Keep it to yourself, and do it in private.
- Do it yourself. This is one task you shouldn't delegate.
- Fire as a last resort.
- Some things we'd fire for "on the spot" include:
  - Dishonesty
  - Any illegal activity such as theft
  - Violent behavior or blatant disregard for the safety of others
  - Substance abuse
  - Sexual misconduct

You can create positive change in your workplace. With the suggestions offered in this chapter, we believe you will be able to hire and keep the best employees. If your goal is to be the best option for your customers, hire the best people so your business can *be* the best.

Key Points Checklist

- ☑ Time spent improving your hiring skills is time well spent.
- ☑ Use the ten-step hiring process to improve the quality of your hiring.
- ☑ Use multiple interviews to get to know the applicants with the most potential.
- ☑ Take time to do it right. You are better off without an employee than with the wrong one.
- ☑ It's not the employees you fire who cause you the most problems; it's the one's you don't fire, even though they deserve to be fired.

Selling Is a Service

Nothing ever happens until somebody sells something.
—RED MOTLEY

A newly hired salesman named Sam Smith wrote his first sales call report back to his boss. The highly successful sales manager was stunned when he read the report because it was obvious that he had hired a man who was nearly illiterate.

Here is what Sam wrote: "Dere Bos; I seen a kumpany which ain't never bot nothin frum us. They sure is nice folks, so I sole them a hunert thousand dolars wurth. I'm goin two Saint Lewis now. Sam."

All that week the sales manager tried to figure out how to fire the new man. Before he could think of a good reason to terminate Sam, he received another sales call report from Saint Louis.

Here is Sam's second report: "Dere Bos; I cum hear and found some grate customurs, so sole them a half a milion dolars wurth. They reely neaded our stuf. I'll trie it hear anuther weak. Sam."

Unsure of what to do, the sales manager consulted with his boss, the company president. The president was a man named Wilson James, who had established a reputation as a tough, but fair leader. Under his management the company had achieved seventeen uninterrupted quarters of growth.

President James read Sam's sales call reports and told the sales manager that he would handle the situation personally. The relieved sales manager sat back to await the firing.

The next day the sales manager received a copy of an e-mail that the president had sent to the entire sales force. Sam Smith's sales call reports were attached to the e-mail.

The president's e-mail read as follows: "Dere sails teem memburs; We ben tryin two hart two spel instead of sel. Plez reed Sellin' Sam Smith's sails call reports and thin let's git on the rode and do like he's dun. Wilson James."

We've met a few "Sellin' Sams" and even hired one or two. But those who reach the pinnacle of sales success are few and far between. More importantly, great salespersons defy stereotypes. Those who seem like naturals often fail, while others who are not so qualified often succeed.

Contrast the "Sellin' Sam" story with the following example of getting the sale and losing the customer.

Peter is the manager of a clothing store in Southern California. He is suave, literate, and has movie-star looks. Peter likes to spend time on the sales floor showing the newly hired sales associates how to sell. He was training a new associate the day this book's coauthor, Don Taylor, visited the store to purchase a new suit. He greeted Don, and asked how he could help. Don told Peter he was looking for a blue suit in a 46 long. Immediately, Peter turned on the charm and turned up the pressure.

During the next fifteen minutes he hovered over Don, handing him suits of various green and brown hues and insisting that he try them on. When Don firmly reminded Peter that he was only interested in a blue suit, Peter lavished Don with praise, telling him he could wear any color, and really should have several colors in his wardrobe.

Finally, Don selected a blue suit with a light gray pinstripe that he liked. While Don was being measured for cuffs, "Pushy Peter" went for the pocketbook. He gathered up a dozen shirts and ties and then insisted that Don allow him to "accessorize" the suit. Several no's later, Peter was still trying.

Don is known to have an easygoing personality and does not anger easily. But this day, Pushy Peter was pushing all the wrong buttons. Finally, in desperation, Don interrupted Peter and said, "I'll take this suit and only this suit. If you won't ring it up now, I'll leave without it."

Selling Is a Service

As you read in the two previous chapters, service is critical to the long-term success of every business. We contend that selling is a critical service process. When that process is executed properly, the results are customers who are more satisfied, spend more money, and are many times more likely to share their good experiences with others.

When you are facing tough competition, it is important to remember four things:

1. The skills and attitudes of every employee will be a large factor in the success or failure of your business. Their selling skills—to provide service and satisfy customers while generating sales—will be a major advantage over the big-box competition.

2. To your customers, the salesperson represents the business. It follows then that if in the minds of your customers the salespeople are good, the business is good. And if the salespeople are bad, so is your business.

3. Selling is as vital to success, as breathing is to life. Robert Lewis Stevenson said, "Everyone lives by selling something."

4. No one wants to be sold anything, but everyone likes to buy.

A Service Example

Frank and Russell decided to open a retail business in a building that Frank owned. They opted to save money by remodeling the store themselves. They decided to Sheetrock the interior walls, though neither of them had any experience hanging or finishing Sheetrock. Both men were bright, hardworking individuals who assumed that putting up Sheetrock wasn't rocket science.

At the local lumberyard, they purchased Sheetrock, nails, plaster, and joint tape. The big 4-by-ten-foot sheets went up fast, and the walls were covered with Sheetrock in two days. Then Frank and Russell began to tape and plaster the seams. They soon learned that getting smooth seams that wouldn't show through the paint wasn't easy. After two exhausting days of taping and sanding, the pair returned to the lumberyard for advice.

They described their project to the clerk and told him of their problems in creating flat seams that could be sanded smooth in a reasonable period of time. The clerk responded with a blank look and an apology that he had never worked with Sheetrock and didn't know how to help. The other young man at the service counter just shook his head and shrugged his shoulders.

Fortunately, a local contractor named Bill overheard the conversation and offered to help. He showed Frank and Russell some tools that would help them create smoother seams that would require less sanding. Bill recommended that they purchase a wire-faced sanding device that had a four-foot handle to make reaching the entire seam easy.

The contractor could have stopped there, and his help would have made Frank and Russell very happy. But Bill knew that service comes before the sale, so he offered to drop by the remodeling project and show them a few application techniques. In thirty minutes he had Frank and Russell making smooth, flat seams. He also shared some finishing tips and gave the pair his card before he left.

With the proper tools and a little technique, Frank and Russell were able to complete the walls in just another day, a savings of many hours of exhaustingly hard work. The store opened on time and was an immediate success. Frank and Russell decided to open a second location. Because of their workload, the pair decided to have most of the work on the second location done by others. Would you like to guess which contractor was selected to do the Sheetrock, paint, and finishing?

This true example has two points. First, the clerks at the lumberyard needed training in the area of product knowledge. Second, the example of Bill the contractor, who went well beyond what was expected, and took time to serve before he attempted to sell. His free service was turned into profit generated by future business and willing referrals.

Missed Opportunities

When you are competing with the power retailers, you cannot afford to allow any potential sales to slip away. In order to grow and prosper, you must capitalize on every selling opportunity. If your promotion seems to be bringing new customers in, but your revenues aren't increasing proportionately, you may have some sales slippage.

There are several reasons why shoppers aren't converted into buyers. Here are seven of the most common missed opportunities:

1. *Lack of Training*. We are convinced that more sales opportunities are missed because front-line contact people aren't properly trained than for any other reason. In fact, the lack of training is probably the root cause of several other missed opportunities in this section. Most successful competitors know that they must train all employees constantly.

2. *Lack of Inventory*. This is a common problem among businesses that aren't competing well. There's an adage that says, "You can't sell out of an empty wagon." We know it is difficult to balance inventory needs with available capital. However, when the inventory level slips below what is satisfactory to the customer, they will often seek alternative buying sources.

   When we see empty shelves and empty shelf facings, we know that at least some of the following conditions exist: the business owner isn't paying attention to inventory movement; cash is tight and the owner simply can't replace the stock because of lack of funds; responsibility has been delegated to others who are not staying on top of restocking; or the restocking source (distributor, vendor, or supplier) isn't reliable.

3. *Apathy*. Apathy is an attitude that is characterized by uncaring indifference and the lack of action. It is a disease that affects the performance of businesses both large and small. Customers tell us that nothing makes them angrier at a business than employees who are uninterested in their needs.

   When your employees aren't providing real selling service, it's not always a lack of knowledge and training. It can also be that you have the wrong people on the front line. If you must choose between an employee who is enthusiastically rambunctious and one who is indifferent, put enthusiasm on your front line every time.

4. *Lack of Product Knowledge.* There are two areas of concern in this often-missed opportunity. The first is salespersons who are ignorant of the products and services they sell, and second, salespersons who don't know the inventory they have available to sell.

   The first area of concern (ignorance) can easily be overcome with knowledge. Salespeople typically have some time on their hands. Instead of reading the newspaper or discussing last night's TV shows, they could be learning about the products they sell.

   The second area of concern (not knowing the inventory) is easily overcome by learning where various product lines and inventory items are displayed. Using spare time to familiarize themselves with the store's inventory can give salespeople confidence in helping customers find exactly what they need quickly.

5. *Misjudging the Customer's Intent to Buy.* Martha Hill and her eighteen-year-old daughter were in the market for a new car. Dressed in Saturday casuals—sweatshirts and jeans—the pair attracted little attention. The usually overaggressive sales force observed their presence and ignored them. The women noticed that when couples or men came on the lot, a salesperson was quick to offer service. Martha and her daughter were offended by the treatment.

   This incident happened nearly ten years ago. The Hills have purchased four vehicles since the snubbing incident, but the dealership that underestimated their intent or ability to buy has never been revisited. Four lost sales due to bad judgment.

6. *Lack of Courtesy.* Thomas Fuller said, "All doors open to courtesy." And we might add that they close quickly to rudeness. Research shows that nearly seven of ten people who stopped doing business with a store or company did so because of the way they were treated.

Small businesses that are trying to compete with the big-boxes can't afford to blow this opportunity to distinguish themselves from the masses. Courtesy, good manners, and politeness cost nothing.

7. *Failure to Suggest "Go With" Items.* When all front-line people are trained to view selling as a service, they begin to anticipate their customer's needs. For example, if a customer in a hardware store buys paint, a savvy salesperson might offer "go with" items such as masking tape, brushes, rollers, drop cloths, or spackling.

We know a small-business owner who sold more than $4,000 worth of Scotch tape in a two-week period just before Christmas, simply by having his checkout clerks ask every customer who purchased wrapping paper if they needed tape. Each clerk had a supply in the checkout area, and when a customer needed tape—more than half did—they pulled out two rolls and said, "Will two rolls be enough, or do you need more?" Nearly all customers bought the offered two rolls.

Here's a challenge for you and your employees. Each week select an item from your inventory, and have everyone come up with the list of "go with" items. Make it a game, get everyone involved, create rewards, and give plenty of recognition for good "go with" ideas. Using this tip can easily add several percentage points to your annual sales growth!

Seven Secrets of Service Selling

1. *Sell with your ears first.* Communications experts agree that with most people there are only two elements of communication: they are either talking or they are getting ready to talk.

This problem has been around a very long time. In 1600, Shakespeare wrote, "Give everyman thine ear, but few thy voice." In 300 B.C., Zeno of Citium stated, "The reason we have two ears and only one mouth is that we may listen more and talk less."

The first key to service selling begins with truly listening to your customers. The goal of service selling is finding out what the customer needs or wants, and then showing them what will most meet their needs and give them value. Sales trainer Ron Willingham illustrates this concept in his book, *The Bestseller!* Willingham says, "Remember . . . you don't talk people into buying; you listen them into buying."

Here are some better listening tips: 1. Focus on the speaker. Make them feel important by giving them your undivided attention. 2. Ask a lot of questions and keep your mouth shut while they are answering. 3. Remember that most folks would rather talk to a brilliant person than listen to one. You begin to build a good relationship by being a good listener.

2. *Understand the customer's viewpoint.* In the service-selling process, there is great value in being able to walk a little in your customer's shoes. Lifelong relationships usually develop when people like each other. To fully understand your customer's perspective, it helps to have an affable and amiable personality. People are much more likely to share their viewpoint with people they like and trust.

When Lee Iacocca was chairman of Chrysler Corporation, he summed up his success in building lasting relationships by saying, "Make someone like you." The results will be invaluable to you in the service-selling process. By listening to your customers and understanding where they're coming from, you can lay a foundation to ensure that you can give them exactly what they want, just the way they want it.

3. *Show the benefit.* The age-old question asked by all customers—usually to themselves—is, "What's in it for me?" Savvy sellers know that the features of a product are not as important as the benefits that features give to the customer. Thomas J. Winninger sums up this concept in his book, *Full Price*, by telling business owners to "focus on what the product does, not what it is."

Perhaps the most important words a service seller ever utters are "The benefit to you is . . . " To connect with your customer every time, you must know your product (service), know your customer, and know the benefits your product or service offers.

4. *Sell the truth*. Trust is an important prerequisite to relationships success. Mark Twain said, "When in doubt, tell the truth." We would add, even when you're not in doubt, tell the truth. People who tell the truth gain both the respect and trust of others.

We believe that owners and employees of small businesses are held to a higher standard of integrity than those of the "monster merchants." We also believe that buyers are becoming more wary of sellers. Therefore, they are more likely to purchase from those businesses they trust.

Ralph Waldo Emerson said, "Truth is the property of no individual, but is the treasure of all men." To retain possession of the truth, you must give it away. It will return to you in the form of trust and service-selling success.

5. *Know your product*. In the process of service selling, you must know what you're selling. We believe that many "also-rans" in the selling profession underestimate the value of product knowledge. As we mentioned in secret number three, knowing your product is the key element in connecting with your customers.

Armed with product knowledge and a thorough understanding of the benefits, a "three-speed, seven-cycle clothes washer" becomes a labor-saving device that gets clothes cleaner, protects delicate garments, saves energy, costs less to operate, and is less harmful to the environment. Know the product, point out the features, and sell the benefits.

Finally, we realize that no human being can know everything about every product. There is no shame in saying, "I don't know," as long as you follow with "But I'll find out." Never say, "I'll find out," without following up.

6. *Underpromise, overdeliver*. Customers expect businesses to keep their promises, that's a given. What they don't expect—and don't often get from the big-boxes—is something extra, some-

thing personal. Here are a few underpromise, overdeliver examples from our own experiences.

- A mechanic not only fixed our car per the estimate and when promised, but also washed the exterior and vacuumed the interior at no charge.

- An appliance dealer who knew the product line helped us make the right choice, and then offered to deliver at a time "convenient to our schedules," instead of "sometime next Tuesday."

- The restaurant owner, who provided a sumptuous meal with attentive service, also brought us a new dessert to try for free.

You can distinguish your business from all others by overdelivering.

7. *Ask for the sale.* Henry Ford once purchased a large insurance policy. One of Ford's close friends was in the insurance business. He was quite upset when he found out about Ford's purchase. He called Ford and asked why Ford hadn't purchased the policy from him. Ford replied, "You never asked me." Savvy service sellers always ask for the sale. Asking for the business doesn't have to include a high-pressure close. Here are a few effective ways to ask for the order that are used by professionals:

- *Insurance Agent*—"This policy will provide the security you desire for your family. Shall I go ahead and write it up for you?"

- *Clothier*—"This suit will resist wrinkling while you travel. Would you like me to have our tailor measure you now?"

- *Appliance Salesperson*—"We have the model you like in stock. Would you like it delivered today?"

- *Professional Speaker*—"I have the date you want available. Shall I book it for you now?"

- *Vacuum Cleaner Salesperson*—"I think we agree that this is the perfect model for your house. Would you like the extended warranty with the unit?"

- *Computer Dealer*—"This laptop has the speed, memory, and software you need. Would you like to take it with you now?"

The common thread in this method of asking for the business is minimal pressure, a reinforcement of the value and benefits, and a required customer response. Don't wimp out at the last minute by saying, "Would you like me to write it up now . . . or do you want to think about it some more?"

Selling to Customer Types

You will improve your success ratio in service selling if you understand some of the basic techniques of selling to different customer types. While we are aware that each customer is different, research shows that there are many common characteristics between customers in easily identifiable groups.

We have identified five groups for which we have provided some "selling to" basics. These tips will help you focus on the specific needs and nuances of each group.

Selling to Women

Females make up more than half of the U.S. population. More than 60 million adult females work outside the home. Women are a formidable market-driving force. In America, they purchase or directly influence the purchase of nearly seven of ten automobiles, make more than 75 percent of health care decisions, make or influence nearly 80 percent of all clothing purchases, and control eight of ten dollars spent on food and household items.

How to Reach Female Consumers

- *Give them respect*. Never assume that a female isn't the decision maker. Treat them as qualified, intelligent, capable buyers, and you won't go wrong.

- *Give them information.* Women typically are well-informed, discerning, and security-oriented. However, most require reinforcement of facts prior to becoming comfortable with the purchase. Stress the benefits, demonstrate the quality, show the value, and make them feel secure.

- *Give them value.* The majority of female buyers say they buy items "when they are on sale." However, women are quick to pay more for quality. Make sure the quality, quantity, and benefits you offer match the price.

- *Give them clean and attractive environments.* Research shows that women are more likely to respond positively to cleaner, warmer, more attractive business environments. We believe that one of the reasons Target took market share from Kmart was the quality of their store environment. Women responded positively to stores with brighter lighting, cleaner floors, and wider aisles by shopping there more frequently. Cleanliness and attractiveness never offend anyone.

- *Give them visuals.* Women shop with their eyes. They visualize how a piece of furniture will look in the den, or how a dress will look at the party. Good merchandising and upscale displays can expedite the selling process.

- *Be kid-friendly.* Female customers are twice as likely to shop with children as men. Take care of the kids, and mom will be happy too. Provide a play area, a video room, or a TV with kids' programming.

- *Use females on your sales force.* Women love buying from women. In typically male-dominated product areas such as furniture, appliances, electronics, automobiles, and tools, well-trained women are often top sales producers.

Selling to Men

There are 74 million adult males in the U.S. workforce. Although they make up the gender minority at 49 percent of the population, they are a potent and sometimes quirky buying force.

How to Reach Male Consumers

- *Show it, and sell it.* Men are visual. Men see what is interesting and important to them. Whether it is an attractive woman, a Corvette, or a Harley Softtail, men seldom miss seeing those things that appeal to them. Who buys TV sets the size of a wall? Men do. Show it to a man, and sell it.

- *Men are tall boys.* They say the only difference between men and boys is the price of their toys. We know grown men who have a basement full of trains, a garage full of fascinating cars, enough tools to have their own TV show, boats the size of a small house, and bicycles that cost as much as a good used car. Sell the boy, and make the man happy.

- *Men are high-tech, high-touch.* Men like the "gee whiz" factor. It can be a hammer with a curved handle or a computer the size of a wallet. Just let men get their hands on it. A man will go to a sporting-goods store for a can of tennis balls, but while he's there he'll try on a ball glove, check out the fishing gear, handle some tennis rackets, and swing a few bats. Let them try it, and they'll buy,

- *Men are macho.* If you want to sell a man, appeal to his manly nature. Men envision themselves as gunfighters, race car drivers, NFL quarterbacks, and lady killers. You won't appeal to a macho man with intellectual superiority or opera music. Talk sports, talk cars, and forget the international chess championship. Sell the man manly stuff.

- *Give them their youth back.* It is said that few women admit their real age, and fewer men act theirs. Men may grow old, but they seldom grow up. This book's coauthor, Don Taylor, drives a 1967 Corvette roadster with 350 horsepower. Why? He says it's because it makes him feel 16 again. Sell to the age he feels, not to the age he is.

- *Sell it now.* Little boys do things on impulse. Big boys buy things on impulse. Be ready to sell when they're ready to buy. It may only take a minute.

Selling to Seniors

Active, healthy, and in general willing to spend, seniors are a very important consumer segment. For our purposes, we will define seniors as all of those born before 1946. The youngest are age 59, and the oldest active seniors are in their late eighties and early nineties. Most are between 60 and 84, and they sport discretionary income that is 50 percent higher than the national average. This group of consumers is nearly 50 million strong, and is often underestimated in terms of their actual buying clout.

How to Reach Senior Consumers

- *Focus on quality.* Seniors remember cars they kept for several years, appliances that stayed around longer than their kids, and furniture that didn't fall apart after three sittings. Sell lasting quality, and enjoy loyal relationships.

- *Sell simplicity.* Seniors grew up with radios with two knobs, refrigerators with one door, clocks with two hands, and no microwave. They now own computers, remote-control devices, digital cameras, and microwaves. They can't set the clocks on their VCRs, they get very frustrated when the computer does anything unusual, and they have trouble programming their microwave. Sell simplicity, and reap satisfaction.

- *Sell fun.* Seniors have worked hard to get where they are today. They value their leisure time, and like to play. Whether retired or working, seniors will buy products and services that add to their quality of life. They travel, enjoy hobbies, and spend on their grandkids. Sell them fun, and enjoy the profits.

- *Sell security.* While this is especially true for those over 70, who experienced the Great Depression or its aftereffects, younger seniors are also security-conscious. They have worked hard to earn the lifestyle they now enjoy, and they don't want it to go away. Minimize their risk, and they will maximize your revenues.

- *Sell young.* Most seniors will not admit to being old. They see themselves as younger, with plenty of life left to live. We know an eighty-year-old great-grandmother who says she likes to go to the senior center so she can help the "old folks." You'll sell more if you show stylish products that are easy to use and do not date themselves as "old." There's money in maturity.

Selling to Baby Boomers

A few months after World War II ended, maternity wards filled up and stayed full for nearly two decades. Between 1946 and 1964, 76 million babies were born in the U.S. The baby boom generation reshaped America. Many social trends, educational expectations, and buying patterns originated with the baby boomers.

This generation caused a generational separation known as the "generation gap." The values, attributes, and actions of baby boomers are radically different from the experience of previous generations of seniors. Today, this group of highly educated, very spoiled, "if it feels good, do it," and "I want it now" consumers earn more, spend more, and borrow more than any previous generation.

How to Reach the Boomers

- *Show them value.* Baby boomers are no different than most consumers: They want good value in exchange for the money they spend. Boomers are strong spenders, but because they are acutely self-interested, they will walk away from any deals with marginal or questionable value. Remember, this is a curious, highly educated segment of the population. They are knowledge-rich. They know products, services, features, and benefits. Often they are more knowledgeable than the person trying to sell them. You can only be successful if you know what you're selling, and focus on giving them honest value.

- *Sell up.* This generation will buy top-of-the-line items. From laptops to lumber, clothing to cars, they like to buy the highest quality. You can benefit if you convert the features of your products and services into tangible benefits that the boomer buyer will receive. So show the best, point out the benefits, and prove why the top-of-the-line is the best value long-term.

- *Don't treat all boomers the same.* This is a diverse generation. Many boomers are enjoying their grandchildren as they turn 50. Others have young children of their own. Some are in the peak of their careers, while others are returning to school or starting a business. Take time to learn about each boomer customer as an individual. This is good advice for all customer groups, but especially wise for this diverse generation.

- *Focus on experience, not age.* Boomers are aging physically, but not mentally. Most are in their forties and fifties, but are still thinking twenties and thirties. They will live longer than any previous generation, and be more active at the same time. They are going to grow old gracefully. Focus your marketing efforts on their experience, not their age. Focus on what they can do, not what they can't. It's a subtle selling philosophy, but a sound one.

- *Understand their limitations.* For example, as boomers age, their eyesight will deteriorate. Make certain your marketing messages can be read. Think about your business cards, brochures, packaging, and so on. You may need to go to larger font sizes, select simpler typefaces, and add more white space. You may need to add a little lighting to brighten your store or office. If you're playing music, turn it down a little. And they'll need a comfortable chair, if they have to wait very long.

- *Don't expect boomers to be traditional buyers.* This is the "different" generation. They shun tradition in their approach to life, business, and buying. They will buy nontraditional goods, they are "early adopters," and they don't care much about the country of origin. Expect the unexpected, and your marketing plans will be successful.

Selling to Generation X

Generation X is the name given to the generation that followed the baby boomers. They are also referred to as the "baby busters." This population segment was born between 1965 and 1978 and range in age from 26 to 39. As a group they have often been maligned and are commonly referred to as the generation of "slackers." This generation lacks the power and sheer size of previous population clusters, but they are truly a generation of their own. They are self-reliant, skeptical, disillusioned, defensive, and sensitive, but they are gaining in the area of income, and they are spenders.

How to Reach Generation X

- *Sell the facts*. Baby busters are skeptical and disillusioned. They are not nearly as trusting and optimistic as previous generations. They require more relationship building prior to developing trust and loyalty. Sell the truth, and build their trust.

- *Build relationships*. This generation feels abandoned. They are latch-key kids, the products of single-parent families, working mothers, and workaholic parents. Relationships, conversation, and just being around others are important to them. Be a friend first, then gain a customer for life.

- *Sell the good life*. Even though they are a small generation, they don't want leftovers. They want everything their parents had, and they want it now. Sell the good life, and sell it now.

- *Sell fun*. Quality-of-life for the baby buster is equated to a high "fun factor." This generation spends big on vacations, toys, and leisure activities. They are still too young to have great worries about their financial future. Sell fun now.

- *Sell change*. Unlike previous generations, generation Xers grew up in the midst of chaos and change. They are comfortable with a fast pace and little stability. They embrace cutting-edge products and services, because it enables them to reject the mind-set and culture of their parents. Sell new, sell different, and sell successfully.

- *Sell independence*. Baby busters are used to being on their own. They have developed instincts and behaviors based on their independence. They may listen to you, but their decisions will be their own. Sell independence to achieve selling success.

- *Sell flexibility.* This generation is not bound to tradition, history, or past. They have few absolutes or unchangeable standards. They are quick to take advantage of newly discovered opportunities and are comfortable with unique approaches to life. Sell flexible opportunities, and reap rewards.

More Selling Tips

Here are a few final thoughts on selling that just didn't seem to fit elsewhere in this chapter. Yet they are just too good not to include.

- Coauthor Don Taylor has a retired college professor, mentor, and friend named Winston D. Stahalecker. Dr. Stahalecker shared this great bit of wisdom: "Great salespersons don't sell anything; they just help customers make the very best buying decisions."

- Never say no to your customer.

- Three sales builders:

   1. *Merchandise "go with" items.* Use your shelf space to sell for you. If you sell paint, be certain to showcase masking tape, drop cloths, brushes, rollers, trim pads, and hand cleaner next to the paint display.

   2. *Suggest "go with" items.* When a customer comes to your checkout area with a CD player, ask if she needs batteries. If he is buying a book, recommend another book by the same author. If she is buying coffee, offer a Danish or a bagel. Challenge yourself to find "go with" items to offer every customer.

   3. *Package "go with" items.* Show the gas can with the lawn mower. Sell the balance and wheel alignment with the new tires. Include the drink with the meal. McDonald's didn't create the "value meal" concept to sell less. You can sell more, too, if you create a package of value.

- Don't focus on what the product is; focus on what it does for the customer.

- If you can't show the benefits, you won't make the sale.

Key Points Checklist

☑ In order to have a great success in the area of service selling, you must excel in three main areas: knowledge, attitudes, and techniques. Remember the acronym KAT:

1. *Knowledge.* Know your products and services, your customers, their needs, your industry, and your competition.

2. *Attitude.* Be friendly, outgoing, confident, helpful, honest, and enthusiastic, and you will find that selling becomes easier.

3. *Techniques.* Develop techniques that enable you to learn your customer's needs, show the benefits, and ask for the business.

☑ Learn the different customer types and how to sell to them.

☑ Remember that selling is a service that enables you to satisfy more customers, generate increased sales, and get positive referrals for future business.

Low-Cost Promotion Strategies

CHAPTER 7

*I know that half the money I spend on advertising is wasted;
but I can never find out which half.*
— JOHN WANAMAKER

Which half indeed? We've heard sad tales and bad tales from enterprising owners of small business who would agree with Wanamaker's words. One appliance store owner told us he had wasted more than $50,000 on advertising before he discovered what worked in his business.

What works well and what does not work at all will depend mostly on *your* business, *your* specific products or services, *your* community, *your* competition, and *your* skills in how *you* promote your business.

One of the questions we're asked most often is, "How much should I spend on advertising?" The answer is, "It depends." That answer alone won't help you decide how much you should budget for promotional activities. So we went to work and created a new self-help tool to enable you to establish a working range for your promotion spending. It's called the Promotion Spending Guide.

You'll find the guide in Chapter Nine, along with other tools to help you compete at a higher level. The Promotion Spending Guide will show you how to analyze your current business condition and practices, your promotion efforts, your competitors, your local media, and your trade area. It will also help you determine a goal for promotion spending.

As you develop promotion ideas, remember to keep these seven important points in mind:

1. Promotion has one primary goal: To get the right message to the right people at the right time.

2. The cheapest promotion you can get is word-of-mouth referrals from your satisfied customers. Keep your current customers happy because it's much less expensive to keep the customers you have than to develop new ones.

3. Great promotion will never make up for inferior quality or poor service.

4. Promotion is an investment in future business.

5. If your promotion doesn't point out benefits for your customer, it's wasted.

6. Promotion is only one element of an effective marketing plan. (Review "The Promotion Factor" in "The Six P's of the Marketing Mix" in Chapter Three.)

7. Promotion does not have to be expensive to be effective.

In this chapter, we offer 101 inexpensive but proven ideas that have worked for thousands of businesses. Some may not apply to your business or industry, but many will help you attract new customers, promote the benefits you offer, and lower your promotion costs. Please feel free to copy them, adapt them, and experiment with them.

101 Low-Cost Promotion Strategies

1. *Invest in good quality, colorful, unique business cards.* Think of your business cards as "mini billboards" that may be the first direct contact a potential customer has with your company. Have some printed for all of your employees and encourage them to pass them out to everyone they meet. This will help build those important relationships between your employees and custom-

ers and will spread the name of your business throughout the community.

Be creative and try for unusual but readable designs. Don't forget to include your phone number and Web address. If a substantial number of your customers are 40 and above, increase the type size to make it easy for older eyes.

2. *Create a good ten-second introduction about yourself and your business.* Make it fifteen to twenty words, and practice it until it rolls off your tongue. For example, when the owner of an auto repair shop passes out his business card, he says, "Hello, I'm Will Jenkins with Jenkins' Automotive. We specialize in finding and fixing problems that no one else can."

3. *Network.* Become active in your community. Like throwing a stone into a pond, your connections with other people will have a rippling effect. One of the best sources of ideas and contacts is to network with others at trade shows, chamber of commerce meetings, and Rotary, Lions, and community functions. Doing so will help you remain competitive and keep you up-to-date on local developments.

When you develop new contacts you will, at the very least, broaden your base of resources for future information. Network for the sake of meeting interesting people—don't cultivate friends and contacts solely for what it will do for you. But remember that networking can also build sales because we all like to do business with people we know.

4. *Develop a clean, crisp, distinctive logo for your business.* Use it on your business cards, letterhead, and invoices, and integrate it throughout your signs and printed materials. A good logo can enhance your business image, increase your name recognition, and create an identity. Use vivid colors and graphics, and make it distinctively yours.

5. *Use every promotion tool at your disposal.* Use your business letterhead, envelopes, return labels, forms, packaging, and invoices to carry your message. Don't underestimate their importance.

With a little thought you can turn your "office supplies" into powerful marketing tools. Mention your commitment to service, quality, and convenience for your customers, or other unique benefits you offer your customers.

6. *Attend trade shows and industry meetings.* One consistent trait of the successful businesspeople we know is that they regularly attend trade shows and meetings related to their business. Away from the everyday duties of running your business, it's the one time when you can make valuable contacts, find new products and suppliers, and find ways to improve your business.

7. *Start a "customer suggestion of the month" program.* Offer a nice gift certificate to the customer whose suggestion is chosen as the best. We would suggest $50 or more. Three good things happen with this type of promotion:

   - You reward present customers (it's a way of saying thanks)

   - You get good suggestions on how to better serve your customers

   - You learn what your customers are thinking

8. *Stage a fun event or happening at your store.* Just about anything you can think of can be used as a theme. With a little creative thinking, you can create an event that will build traffic and generate free publicity. Team up with local celebrities, media representatives, and even other business owners.

9. *Start a club.* The keys to forming a successful club are to make sure it's fun, involve the members from its inception, offer adequate rewards for membership (discounts, preferred customer mailings, etc.), keep in close contact with the members, and solicit their input.

10. *Write an article for a trade publication.* Select publications catering to your field of expertise, and take a close look at the types of articles they run. Make sure your article fits the format. Call the editors or associate editors with specific questions about their

guidelines and what sorts of photographs (if any) should accompany the article. To build your credibility and name recognition, post reprints of the article in your store or send it to your mailing list.

11. *Invite everyone you do business with to do business with you.* We know a menswear shop that has business cards printed with an offer of a discount on the reverse side of the card. The owner asks every employee to hand out his or her cards, and offers an incentive for doing so.

    Employees pass out business cards to everyone they do business with and say, "Shop with us." At the end of each quarter, the owner pays a bonus to the employee who has had the most cards returned. One employee's bonus was $500, and store sales increased by more than $13,000 that quarter.

12. *Package a slow-moving item with a fast seller to move out the former.* Keep in mind that your "slow mover" must be a real value or it will slow sales of fast-moving items.

13. *Develop a customers mailing list.* Use a computer for this to eliminate most of the hassle. By having an accurate mailing list, you'll open doors to all sorts of marketing possibilities.

14. *Steal and adapt good ideas from others.* The legends of retailing all were cat burglars of good ideas. Buy out-of-town papers and scan the ads for design ideas. Look closely at direct mail pieces you receive. Any ideas there? Visit the stores of your competitors and notice what they're doing and the things they're advertising. Watch big companies and small companies to see what tactics they are using to promote their businesses. The key words are *steal* and *adapt*.

15. *Become an expert on a subject involving your business.* Communicate your expertise to radio and TV talk show hosts, newspaper editors and columnists, magazine publishers, and other public figures. You may be called upon for a quote for a publication or program that can mean big-time publicity for you and your company.

16. *Always say "thank you" either verbally or in writing.* Showing your appreciation to current customers will help make them future customers. In a world that has become very impersonal, a handwritten thank-you card makes a lasting impression.

17. *Send birthday and anniversary cards.* Most of us like to be recognized on our special days. (A client mentioned to us that the card he got from the appliance store he patronizes was the only birthday card he received.) Offer customers a discount if they bring the card in during a specified time period or let them know there's a special gift waiting for them.

18. *Use "messages on hold" to carry your advertising message via the telephone.* These can be great to advertise your special services, or the expertise of your employees. The added benefit for the customers who must be placed on hold is that they hear the message *you* want them to. We know store owners who switched to their own customized "messages on hold" when customers mentioned they heard a competitor's advertisement while listening to the radio that was being played through the telephone.

19. *Exhibit at trade shows or community fairs.* You're looking for exposure and sales. Take advantage of the opportunity to acquaint prospective customers with what you have to offer. Be creative with your displays and have a drawing for a free product or gift certificate to your store. Capture the names for your mailing list.

    Many communities have "business-to-business expos" where a variety of businesses can display their products and advertise their services. If you don't have such a program, talk to your chamber of commerce and try to organize one.

20. *Send "special event notes or cards" congratulating customers for a promotion, accomplishment, graduation, or other special event.* Ask your employees to keep their ears tuned to conversations and assign an employee to daily scan the newspaper for news about your customers that might merit a congratulatory note.

21. *Sponsor a drawing for free merchandise.* Entry forms could be a brief questionnaire capturing essential information such as names and addresses (which will tell you where your customers come from) and also information about whether they intend to purchase the type of product you sell within the next sixty days. You'll get valuable information to help you target your advertising.

22. *Donate your services or products to a nonprofit organization for a fund-raiser or special event.* Putting your name and your products in front of the public will have a positive effect and show you are a supporter of your community.

23. *Host how-to classes or seminars.* Such strategies are widely used by the retail giants. Home Depot and Lowe's regularly host free clinics on topics related to do-it-yourself projects. Sewing machine retailers offer free "how to" classes to machine purchasers and prospects. Lawn and garden centers offer free landscaping courses. The key is to provide useful information and show how what you sell can improve quality of life for your customers.

24. *Send a note or letter to someone whose work you admire.* It's always nice for people to hear a word of praise. The benefits are that you build rapport and may build business, since we all like to be associated with people who are doing more than just peddling their wares.

25. *Use promotion partners.* Seek out informal partnerships with noncompeting businesses and arrange to work together in mutually beneficial ways. You can exchange coupons for distribution, business cards, or sample products.

26. *Use as much co-op advertising money as you can.* Take advantage of the matching funds that manufacturers, distributors, and suppliers often offer to help you advertise their products. By some estimates, as much of 50 percent of co-op allocations aren't being used.

    Be sure to use your logo, keep the name and image of your

business prominent in the advertisement, and comply with all the co-op regulations. Some of the record-keeping requirements may be time-consuming, but it will make your advertising dollars go further.

27. *Find out if any of your suppliers have "vendor money" available.* Vendor money differs from co-op money in that it can be tailored to your promotion needs. Co-op advertising is usually tied to specific times, products, and parameters.

28. *Develop an effective yellow page ad.* Many small-business owners develop their yellow page ad using the basic format suggested by the sellers of yellow page advertising. While this approach may be adequate, it won't make you stand out from the other ads, particularly if you're in a very competitive market. (Remember that one of the rules is "attract attention.")

    Get ideas by going to the library and looking at yellow page ads in some out-of-town phone books. When you travel out of town, do the same thing.

    Look at the ads of your competitors and then make sure yours is different. People turn to the yellow pages to discover specific information, so give it to them—lots of it. List what you offer (products, services, and benefits), grab their attention with a strong headline, and use graphics or a photograph.

29. *Investigate remnant space advertisements.* This is advertising space in regional editions of national publications "left over" after major advertisers have bought space. Magazines are put together in four-page units, and sometimes not enough ads will be sold to fill the unit, so remnant space is sold very cheaply to fill the section. Call the advertising department of the magazine directly, well in advance of the publication date.

30. *Find a way to connect your products or services with a famous person or local personality.* Skiers have raised this tactic to an art form. Right after coming down the slope, the first thing they do is pull off their skis and pose, the name of the skis prominently shown. Wouldn't you love to have your name so prominently exhibited?

Keep tabs of interesting or famous people who will be visiting your town or find someone who's doing something that's bound to get media attention. Invite them to come to your store and, with their permission, notify the press.

31. *Offer free services to add value to the products you sell.* This one element can be the deciding factor in whether a customer decides to buy from you or from your competition. Appliance dealers might offer free delivery and free hookups. Gift shops can provide free gift-wrapping and free delivery.

32. *Make a long-lasting impression with specialty advertising* (caps, writing instruments, calendars, mugs, paperweights, note pads, etc.). Two big advantages of using this medium are that your name stays in front of the consumer a long time, and if chosen well, your advertising can generate a good response because everyone loves a useful, attractive free gift.

    There are thousands of different types of specialty advertising. Whatever type you chose, make sure to imprint your logo, name, and address, and be sure to keep your selection relevant to your business and appropriate for your customer. Your image is at stake: Select items that are durable, high quality, and useful.

33. *Offer something for free.* A music store might offer free lessons with every guitar purchase. A restaurant might offer a free dessert with every entrée. Never underestimate the pulling power of "free."

34. *Find a win/win opportunity to become a civic partner.* Service clubs and organizations, PTAs, churches, and school groups are all targets for joint promotions. The key is to find a partnership where everyone benefits and then gain the support of all the players involved.

35. *Offer progressive reductions.* The owner of a Missouri garden center was overstocked with garden tractors and displayed one of them in his store in a front window location. He promised to

reduce the price by $10 every day until it sold. The local radio station picked it up as a news story, and every day, the disc jockeys asked, "How low will it go?"

Shortly after the tractor sold, other customers came in offering to buy the tractor at that day's price, which the owner was happy to do with the remaining tractors. This strategy generated interest and cleared inventory.

36. *Start a frequent buyer program by copying the airlines' frequent flyer programs.* For small-business owners, this type of program offers incentives for loyal customers to continue to buy from you and rewards them for doing so. The "prize" might be a discount, or their next item free, depending on the products or services you sell. One of the ways to build your business is to get your current customers to buy more from you.

37. *Set up merchandise displays in nearby vacant buildings.* Many cities have vacant buildings badly in need of tenants, or at least decoration. By displaying your products in these facilities, you reduce the ugliness of empty buildings and promote your business much like a billboard. The display must reflect positively on your business, so make sure your display is attractive, with a nice background. Include a big sign with your business name and address.

38. *Create a killer business presentation.* The owner of a bus leasing company charters his bus for special trips. To promote the service, he created a funny, entertaining slide show that was so well done, he's had many requests to present the program to service clubs. The audience enjoyed the entertainment, and it brought great exposure to the company—all at no cost.

39. *Use unlikely promotion spaces.* For example, a clothier might use his or her dressing rooms, or all types of businesses can use their restrooms to promote unadvertised specials, to post current advertising, and to reinforce your mission statements.

40. *Set up truly unusual displays in your store windows.* If they're zany, unique, or interesting enough, they may attract enough local

interest to be newsworthy. Mechanized or moving displays are highly memorable.

41. *Create a float for your local parade.* Whether it's for July 4th, homecoming, your city's birthday celebration, or the kickoff event for your county fair, parades can be a great way to get exposure for your business. If you try this idea, make the float unique and memorable.

42. *Sponsor or cosponsor a race or event such as a bike-a-thon or walk/ run.* These events, if promoted well, can attract a lot of attention. Those who participate will link your business to a worthwhile cause. Well ahead of time, discuss promotion plans with event organizers and request a copy of the names and addresses of participants for your mailing list. The benefits will be twofold: You'll build name recognition and show your community spirit.

43. *Sponsor or cosponsor a sports team.* Have your name printed— possibly with your slogan—on the back of the shirts. Whether it's your son's baseball team, your daughter's soccer team, or an employee's volleyball team, you'll earn appreciation and recognition with the sponsorship.

44. *Draw people into your store with a fun contest.* Whether it be a pumpkin-carving contest in the fall, guessing the date of the first winter snowfall, or coming closest to the hour and minute an ice sculpture will melt down in August, contests can generate fun, traffic, and publicity.

45. *Enter contests.* Associations, chambers of commerce, and a variety of other organizations offer contests in many fields. Investigate the qualifications and apply for the ones that fit you and your business.

   Winners are often honored with concrete evidence that they are the best in the field. This can really boost your marketing efforts. The story may get picked up by local or national publications, ever widening your sphere of influence. Don't miss this opportunity on the local—or broader—level to boost your image.

46. *Send postcards.* A specialty coffee and tea company sends customers a postcard when they haven't shopped or ordered in a while. It's an attractive, handwritten card that is addressed directly to the customer and says simply, "We haven't seen you in a while. Let us know if you need anything." Postcards can carry seasonal messages, announced special sales, or just say thank you.

47. *Plan a festive holiday party.* It's a nice way to say, "Thanks for your business," while generating sales. You can celebrate traditional holidays such as Christmas, Hanukkah, Fourth of July, Labor Day, and so on, or you can make up your own. You can serve wine and cheese, punch and cookies, or ice cream and cake. It's a party. The little town of Shamrock, Texas, capitalizes on its name with a St. Patrick's Day celebration that includes nearly all businesses and residents.

48. *Throw a birthday party for your company.* Every business has a starting (birth) date. Make it a reason to celebrate. Invite everyone, especially your best customers.

49. *Make full use of a toll-free hot line or support line.* Building long-term customer relationships is what modern-day customer service is all about, and one way that all types of businesses are discovering they can do this with out-of-town customers is to keep in touch via a toll-free line. Do your customers know that you'll always be available to answer their questions about the products they buy from you? It's a great selling point and a good way to turn them into lifetime customers.

50. *Send messages to your customers via the fax,* but get their permission first. We believe that providing useful tips and information, offering special "fax only" discounts, and giving customers "news they can use" is a sound way to promote your business.

51. *Preprogram your fax or computer/fax to send press releases directly to media contacts.* You never know what the media will pick up on a slow news day.

52. *Be the first.* One drugstore owner in Alabama was the first to offer free screenings for blood pressure and blood sugar, and the first with free delivery of prescriptions. It's one way to differentiate your business from the competition, and a way to make an important and lasting impression on your customers.

53. *Provide tip sheets for your customers.* These can include instructions on how to install a faucet (a hardware business), how to plant a perennial garden (garden center), or how to take care of your new Guinea pig (pet store). The new breed of customer is hungry for information. Give it to them.

54. *Volunteer for high-visibility assignments such as making presentations, chairing committees, or organizing events.* Being visible in the community through such activities will make you visible in the marketplace. Everyone likes to do business with people they know and respect. (Don't overdo this one. Your focus must never stray too far from running your business.)

55. *Write a letter to the editor or do a guest editorial.* This can be a dynamic marketing device if you communicate well and can offer a reasonable solution, instead of just articulating the problem. Presenting yourself well in the newspaper will help you gain some respect as a person who is taking a leadership and advocacy position on an important topic of local interest. Pay attention to the publication's format and guidelines, and write clearly and concisely. Laminate or frame the printed piece, and display it in your store. Avoid politics.

56. *Send your customers to each other.* It is important to ask for referrals, but you should also give referrals. Send them with a message such as, "Mary Abbott suggested I come to see you." In one-to-one marketing, what goes around comes around.

57. *Forward articles of interest to your customers and prospects.* Taking time to share important knowledge shows your thoughtfulness as well as your understanding of your customers' needs.

58. *Use car door signage.* Magnetic car door signs can be moved from vehicle to vehicle and can carry your message to the traffic

masses. If appropriate, use a teaser such as "Ask me about how to save money on your car insurance." Always include your Web address on signs.

59. *Give customers the royal treatment.* One financial planner we know hires a limousine and driver to pick up and return prospects for their initial consultation. There was a dramatic drop in no-shows! Talk about making a lasting first impression.

60. *Mail out oversized postcards suitable for company bulletin boards.* Send a "quote of the month," "a motivational adage," or a "business cartoon." If you do this well, some of these will be saved for years.

61. *Hit the rubber chicken circuit.* Local civic clubs and associations are always looking for good, entertaining, and informative programs. Your chamber of commerce may have a list of local organizations. Develop a professional-looking letter or flyer offering your services, and send it to the program chairperson. Take along your business cards.

    If you lack the confidence to do public speaking, join your local Toastmasters club. They will help you overcome your fears, and their first manual will give you the basics of preparing a good presentation.

62. *Adopt a unique day for your company's promotion.* All retailers use traditional holidays for promotion, so do something different.

    For example, an Ohio CPA firm does a strong marketing campaign using May 7th as their unique day. What's special about May 7th? That is the day when the average American has earned enough to pay all their taxes. The rest of the year they are working for themselves. The CPA firm uses the theme: We can help you move this day earlier in the year.

63. *Use list and database mailing firms.* If you've got a great idea for a mailer, you can supplement your own mailing list by purchasing lists of names from list companies. If you purchase a list of 5,000 names, but only plan to mail out 1,000 pieces, consider

using the bottom of the list. These people receive fewer mailings than those at the front of the alphabet.

64. *Explore local and regional editions of national publications for lower ad rates.* Example: An ad in the national edition of *TV Guide* can cost up to $100,000, but purchasing a local edition ad may only cost a few hundred dollars.

65. *Produce a simple instructional video.* A Texas-based manufacturer of portable oil change systems created a short video to show prospective customers how easy it is to use their system. Now prospects can see how they can save time and money with the Oil Vac unit. Sales have more than doubled each of the last two years.

66. *Develop a fax cover sheet that sells.* Use it to promote a monthly special or point out a benefit of doing business with you. Change it often, and have some creative fun with it.

67. *Offer fax and online ordering.* Many retailers are building sales by allowing customers to order from their homes or workplaces. One office products supply company has made it easy for customers to order by fax or via the Internet. They promise next-day delivery for items ordered before 5 P.M. Each order is packaged the evening before and delivered as early as possible the following day. Sales are up dramatically despite having both Office Depot and Office Max in their trade area.

68. *Develop a Web site based on the IEE formula.* Make it *Informative, Entertaining,* and *Ever-changing.* A good Web site can boost your credibility, generate sales, and work for you twenty-four hours per day all year long.

69. *Cross-promote.* Once your site is developed, and you are happy with it, promote it in all of your other advertising efforts. Put it on your business cards, letterhead, invoices, and advertising. Remember, the goal of promotion is to get the right message to the right person at the right time. You never know, when you're

cross-promoting, who will respond to what message at what time.

70. *Think in terms of customer clusters.* A local weight loss clinic hit the jackpot with a mailing sixty days prior to the local high school's annual class reunion. The flyer simply said, "Lose 15 pounds before you see all your old classmates." More than thirty people signed up for the special diet/exercise clinic.

71. *Create a business "tag line."* A good tag line, used consistently, can help establish your business identity and make your business memorable. Who can forget Wendy's "Where's the Beef?' or Nike's "Just do it!"? Here are some we like: A tent rental company, "We've got you covered." An apartment complex, "A great place to call home." A lumberyard, "Quality made us famous—service made us grow." A coffee company, "Something's always brewing." A photography shop, "We make memories."

72. *Create a two-way merchant coupon network.* With this inexpensive promotion, noncompeting businesses agree to hand out each other's coupons. For example, a restaurant could exchange coupons with a local dry cleaner. A transmission repair shop could exchange with a tire retailer. A network of several business owners can be established and the coupon exchange rotated regularly between members.

73. *Hold a business card drawing.* A leather goods retailer offers a free briefcase every month to customers who drop off their business cards. The cards are collected in the briefcase, which has a sign that says, "Win this briefcase." This business generates hundreds of leads each year at a total cost of less than $300.

74. *Offer a "bring a friend incentive."* Want to find new customers? Encourage your existing customers to bring a friend who has never been to your business. Remember from Chapter Four that a lifetime customer can be worth thousands, so make the reward something nice. A motorcycle dealership offers a $250 dollar

gift certificate good toward the purchase of any motorcycle in stock. A trendy café offers free dessert for both parties when a first-time customer is brought in.

75. *Hold a customer appreciation day.* The owners of a local butcher shop hold an annual hamburger cookout to say thanks to their customers. Soft drinks are provided by the local bottler, buns by a nearby bakery, and condiments by a local grocery store—all in exchange for the free publicity the event generates. Customers love it, and many first-time contacts are made each year.

76. *Do a neighborhood marketing blitz.* Send your employees out with business flyers and inexpensive free gifts and have them blitz the neighborhood. If no one is home, have them leave the door hangers with the offer of a free gift that can be picked up at your business.

77. *Use shelf talkers to power up in-store sales.* Shelf talkers are little signs that attach to your merchandise displays. They contain simple wording such as: "Try me!" "New, low price!" "Buy two, and save!" "$1 off!" and so on.

78. *Use signs to suggest "go with" items.* A paint store uses signs to set on top of one-gallon paint buckets that remind customers about related sales items. For example, " 'Don't forget the masking tape!" "Need rollers? 3-pack for $3." "Drop cloths $1.99." Suggestive selling is a great way to increase sales while helping remind the customer of needed items.

79. *Use carryout bags to carry a marketing message.* Print your tag line on the bags you provide for your customer's convenience. A gift shop uses a bag geared to special holidays. For example, in October through December the bags have gift suggestions for mom. Each bag has a list of ten gift ideas.

80. *Try punch cards to increase loyalty and frequency.* Punch cards are wallet-size cards that offer the cardholder something in return for buying a certain number of items from your business. The card is punched with each purchase. A pet-store owner offers a

free bag of dog food after a purchase of ten bags. An ice cream store offers a free cone after the purchase of eight. Have your employees ask each customer if they have a punch card.

81. *Use the back of your business card as a coupon.* Most business cards are blank on the back side. Savvy business owners often use their cards as a handwritten coupon. The owner of a miniature golf complex has his son (a teenager) pass out signed cards offering a free game of miniature golf. Each card given out averages a return of 2.3 paid rounds. Nobody likes to play by himself.

82. *Use a marriage mailer.* Marriage mailers are multiple ad/coupon mailers where two or more merchants add a piece to the mailer. Each business pays for its own printing, adds 200 names to the common database, and shares the cost of postage. Everyone gets the advantage of big savings and new potential customers.

83. *Use signs as silent salesmen.* A good sign is a hard worker who shows up every day and never calls in sick. It doesn't require commission or benefits and can increase sales on point-of-purchase displays by as much as 24 percent. Signing tips: Be brief, be specific, list benefits, show savings, explain what isn't obvious.

84. *Use signs to stretch your advertising dollars.* Create signs that say, "As advertised." If something is important enough to advertise, it deserves a sign. One store owner admitted to using this technique to match the prices of his competitor's ads. He just doesn't say who did the advertising.

85. *Use stickers.* Inexpensive stick-on labels will remind your customers about you long after the sale. Use your company logo, tag line, and contact information. An outdoor power equipment dealer places a high-quality sticker on every mower, tiller, and garden tractor he sells. He can track several sales to neighbors of former customers who saw the sticker.

86. *Turn adversity into a promotion.* A music store owner saw traffic drop by 30 percent when the highway department embarked on

a street-widening project in front of his store. He created a contest and offered a guitar as a prize for the person who came the closest to guessing the exact day when the street project would be finished. He called it "making the best of a bad situation."

87. *Turn awards and accomplishments into publicity.* When a local business was named the "top small business of the year" by its local Chamber of Commerce, the owner wrote a press release and provided additional interesting but little-known information about his business. This savvy owner turned a nice award into three local media follow-up stories and a feature article in his trade magazine.

88. *Send out a quality newsletter on a regular basis.* Newsletters can be prime vehicles for conveying useful information, welcome tips, and news about your business. Create your newsletters with the customer in mind. Pack it with useful information, and your readers will look forward to receiving it each time.

89. *Don't ignore the kids.* Children and young adults play an increasing role in the purchasing decisions of their parents. A family dentist has video games for kids to play while waiting for their appointment. A children's clothing store has a play area complete with a two-story playhouse and toys. Keep the kids happy, and mom and dad are happy to.

90. *Create your own name badges.* Use a bright, creative shape with your store logo and your name and big bold letters. Even at events where name tags are furnished, you can stand out from the crowd with your own custom name badge.

91. *Use multiple stamps on your direct mailings.* It sounds quirky, but it works. You still have to apply the same amount of postage, but you create a unique look that separates you from all of the bulk mail stamps. First-class mail is 37 cents as of this writing, so you could use three ten-cent stamps, a five, and a two. Your letters are much more likely to be noticed and opened.

92. *Offer employees SPIFS.* SPIFS are "special incentives for sales." A hardware owner arranged a truckload buy of brand-name

fertilizer and saved more than $1.50 per bag. He gave employees a SPIF on every bag they sold and carried out for the customer. Overall store sales went up more than 17 percent over the previous years, and the four employees earned an average SPIF bonus of more than $300 the first month. A spiffy deal all around.

93. *Turn your delivery vehicles into rolling billboards.* What's more visible than a highway billboard? A rolling billboard that promotes your business wherever it goes and wherever it is parked. Full-color graphics are getting less expensive every day. You can have a Liberace look on a Ben Franklin budget.

94. *Coach smiles.* Nothing reassures first-time customers more than your front-line contact people who know how to smile. Smiles and friendly personalities make people feel welcome. Comfortable shoppers spend more money. One retailer vows that his best promotion strategy was to encourage his employees to smile.

95. *Provide product demonstrations.* We're amazed at how people will turn out for product demonstrations. Sewing machine dealers bring in "vendor" experts to demonstrate the latest sewing techniques. Power tool suppliers have "how-to-use-it" shows. Chainsaw manufactures bring in chainsaw wood carvers to demonstrate their product's capabilities. Talk to your vendors and suppliers, or just do it yourself.

96. *Use stuffers.* You can insert advertising stuffers into shoppers' bags at the point of purchase, or mail them with your monthly statements. You can use coupons, consumer tips, sales notices, or even customer-service questionnaires.

97. *Use the pulsing technique.* Political organizations have been using this technique for years to stretch their media budget. The pulsing technique saturates a medium (radio for example) for a few days and then lays out of the market for a few days. Then saturates it again, and then lays out again. Even though fewer dol-

lars are spent, the listening public remembers the pulses, not the quiet time. The result is higher awareness and better response.

98. *Have a private sale.* Send out high-quality invitations inviting past customers to a "by invitation only" sale. Hold the sale at a time when your business is normally closed. Offer discounts and packages-of-values that are good only at the private sale. One appliance dealer told us he has sold as much as $100,000 worth of appliances in a private one-day event.

99. *Try a classified ad.* A surprising number of people read the classified ads regularly. Keep the ad short and simple. Try several different ads to find those that generate the best response rates.

100. *Create a shared catalog.* A twelve-page, full-color, glossy catalog can be utilized by six different merchants, and each would share the cost. The front and back covers can feature all the merchants involved in the catalog, and each merchant receives two pages inside. Published in large numbers, the catalog can be produced for pennies per unit. Catalogs can be used as newspaper inserts or freestanding mailings, or just given out at your store.

101. *Create a Web site "tip of the week."* A lawn and garden center might offer tips on gardening, lawn care, and proper planting of trees and shrubs. These tips could be seasonal in nature, and encourage the proper use of supplies available from the garden center. A bookstore might offer a suggested reading list featuring the newest best-sellers and books of local interest.

Key Points Checklist

☑ Promotion does not have to be expensive to be effective.

☑ The goal of promotion is to get the right message to the right people at the right time.

☑ Great promotion does not make up for poor quality or inferior service.

☑ The Promotion Spending Guide will help you match your promotion spending to your business environment. (See Chapter Nine.)

Knowledge Is Power

CHAPTER 8

It's what you learn after you know it all that counts.
—JOHN WOODEN

The more you know about your business, the more likely you are to survive and prosper. When you understand how to use the information your company generates, you can increase your earning power, raise your standard of living, and strengthen your business.

Every successful company we've interviewed gathers and analyzes management information regularly. It's not just a habit or a routine. It is the foundation of their decision-making process. Good decisions require good information.

We will cover three types of information in this chapter:

1. Financial information

2. Customer information

3. Productivity and efficiency information

You Can't Manage Numbers You Don't Have

Sound financial management is based on facts, not feelings. When you have good numbers (facts), you will be able to plan, organize, and control what has to be done. Financial management will help you trim expenses, eliminate waste, grow your profits, and save on income taxes.

When we started our first business, our initial financial system was simple. It consisted of a medium-sized cardboard box and a checkbook. We deposited all invoices, receipts, bills, and other paperwork in the box. We paid our bills out of the checkbook.

During the first several months, everything went smoothly. Then, near the end of the first year, the box got full about the same time our checking account hit empty. We knew we had a problem, but didn't know what it was. Attorney and corporate executive Owen D. Young described us well. He said, "It is not the crook in modern business we fear but the honest man who does not know what he is doing."

Records Are Vital

Records are the groundwork you need to successfully build your business. You must have good records to create accurate financial statements. *You must have accurate, timely financial statements to make good decisions.* It follows then that good records are vital to good decision making.

However, there are several other valid reasons for keeping accurate records in addition to making good business decisions. These include:

- The Internal Revenue Service requires you to keep records for tax purposes.

- Accurate, up-to-date records are a prerequisite for borrowing money from a financial institution.

- You can use your records to uncover waste and internal shrinkage (theft).

- Records provide the basics for measuring effectiveness and efficiency.

- Accurate records aid in tracking trends.

- Accurate records help you find problems while they are still small.

First you should determine if your record-keeping system will provide all of the information you need, when you need it. This information is critical because you cannot manage numbers you don't have.

Back to the Basics

The late Vince Lombardi was a professional football coach whose teams always excelled in mastering the basic functions of the game. Once after a humiliating loss to the Chicago Bears, Lombardi called a rare Monday morning meeting for his team, the Green Bay Packers. He told them quietly that they needed to get refocused on the basics. He then held up a football and said, "Gentlemen, this is a *football*."

Even if you are a veteran business owner, please bear with us as we review a few basics. Like a good football play, your records must be *simple, timely, accurate, relevant,* and *consistent.*

There are at least seven basic sets of records or journals that you should maintain. Some businesses may require additional information for management or reporting purposes, but usually this information is enough to start with.

1. *A Sales Journal.* The sales journal is a record of revenue coming into your business. You can divide revenue into several categories, such as different product lines, services, suppliers, and geographic areas.

2. *An Expense Journal.* The expense journal is a running record of all expenses incurred in the normal process of doing business. We suggest that you pay all bills by check and let your checkbook register act as a backup for this journal. Organize expenses into common groups such as wages, payroll expenses, utilities, advertising, rent, supplies, and repairs.

3. *An Accounts Receivable Schedule.* Accounts receivable are monies you haven't collected for products or services already sold and delivered. Your accounts receivable schedule should record each credit sale by customer name, date, the product sold or service rendered, and the dollar amount. You can maintain this list for current accounts (those unpaid for thirty days or less) and past-due accounts (those unpaid for thirty days or more). We will discuss managing your accounts receivable later in this chapter.

4. *An Accounts Payable Schedule.* This schedule is a list of suppliers and others to whom your business owes money. It is a running record that tracks to whom, for what, how much, and when the money is due.

5. *A Payroll Journal.* Monthly, quarterly, and yearly payroll reports are required by many state agencies and the federal government. The payroll journal is a single source to record all applicable information regarding your employees' earnings. This journal allows you to record all regular and overtime pay, Social Security taxes, federal income taxes, Medicare taxes, state income taxes (where applicable), earned income credits, federal unemployment taxes, and state unemployment taxes (where applicable).

6. *A Fixed-Asset Schedule.* The IRS recognizes that the tangible assets of a business—buildings, equipment, vehicles, furniture, fixtures, and so on—may wear out or decline in value—that is, depreciate—over time. They allow business owners to calculate the decrease in value, or depreciation, and to deduct it from their earnings.

    To ensure that all deductions are taken properly, you need to keep records of when assets are purchased, the type of asset (buildings, vehicles, equipment, and so on), and the original purchase price. Calculating the amount of depreciation you can deduct from your net income can be complex, and we recommend that you involve a professional in the process.

7. *An Owner's Journal.* The owner's journal is a record of money that the owner(s) of a sole proprietorship or some partnerships have put into or taken out of the business.

Pouring Your Financial Foundation

Once you have recorded all of the financial transactions for a period in the proper journals and schedules, it is time to bring these ingredients together. Like sand, gravel, water, and cement mix together to make concrete, your records can be mixed together to form financial statements.

These statements, when properly formed, become the foundation of your financial decision making. Nearly every decision you make for your business will have financial impact. For example, if you wish to try a new, aggressive promotion strategy, you'll need to know if you have the cash to support it. If you want to expand with borrowed capital, you'll need to prove to the lender that you can repay the debt from profits generated.

There are three financial statements every business should create on a regular, timely basis. These statements are:

- The profit-and-loss (or income) statement

- The balance sheet

- The cash flow statement

Your financial statements work together as a unit. All three are required to create a complete financial picture of your business.

The Profit-and-Loss (or Income) Statement

The profit-and-loss statement is more commonly called an income statement, and that is how we will refer to it throughout the remainder of this chapter. The income statement is a composite or summary of a company's sales and expenses over a specific period of time. It should be prepared at least monthly. The income statement is established according to a system of rules known as Generally Accepted Accounting Principles (GAAP). These rules apply to all businesses, large or small. Income statements follow the general format shown in Exhibit 8-1.

Exhibit 8-1. A simplified income statement for a retail store.

Canyon Heights Hardware
Income Statement for Month Ended January 31, 2005

Net Sales		$74,000
Cost of Goods Sold		58,000
Gross Profit		$16,000
Operating Expenses		
Wages	$6,400	
Rent	1,800	
Payroll Expense	850	
Advertising	600	
Insurance	450	
Interest	300	
Supplies	200	
Miscellaneous	670	
Total Expenses		$11,270
Total Net Income		$ 4,730

The Balance Sheet

The balance sheet provides a record of the financial health of your company as of a certain date. It is a snapshot of your business at that point in time.

The balance sheet shows the book value of your business and contains two main sections. The first is a record of assets, which includes anything the business owns that has monetary value. The second is a statement of liabilities and owner's equity.

On the balance sheet, total assets must equal the combined totals of the liabilities and owner's equity. Expressed as an equation: *Assets = Liabilities + Owner's Equity*. The assets—items the business owns—are listed in two main categories: current assets and long-term, or fixed assets.

Current assets are those that can be readily converted into dollars through your normal business cycle. These include cash, accounts receivable, and inventory.

Long-term, or fixed, assets are not readily converted to cash and have usefulness to the business over longer periods of time. Long-term assets include items such as buildings, land, vehicles, equipment, and furniture.

The liabilities—what the business owes—are also listed in two main groups: current liabilities and long-term liabilities.

Current liabilities are the short-term financial obligations of your business that are payable within one year. Examples would include accounts payable, taxes, current portion of long-term debt, and short-term loans.

Long-term liabilities are all debts not due for payment within one year. These would include the noncurrent portion of all loans on your land and buildings, equipment loans, and mortgages.

The difference between the total assets (the value of what the business owns) and the total liabilities (what the business owes) is known as the "owners equity" or the "net worth" of the business. Sometimes the level of debt exceeds the value of the assets, and the owner has a negative equity position or a minus net worth.

Exhibit 8-2 is a sample balance sheet. Note that the assets are grouped at the top of the balance sheet, and the liabilities and owner's equity are listed on the bottom half. The categories and format of the balance sheet also follow GAAP.

Exhibit 8-2. A typical balance sheet for a small retail store.

Borger Bargain Barn
Balance Sheet December 31, 2004

Current Assets:			
Cash	$ 1,500		
Accounts Receivable	2,500		
Inventory	78,000		
Total Current Assets		$82,000	
Fixed Assets:			
Building	$68,000		
Furniture and equipment	12,000		
Vehicles	10,000		
Total Fixed Assets		$90,000	
TOTAL ASSETS			$172,000
Current Liabilities:			
Accounts Payable	$18,000		
Notes Payable	24,000		
Current Portion Long-Term Debt	6,500		
Total Current Liabilities		$48,500	
Long-Term Liabilities:			
Mortgage Payable (Building)	$45,000		
Notes Payable (Vehicle)	6,500		
Total Long-Term Liabilities		$51,500	
Owner's Equity:			
Barry Barnes, Owner	72,000		
Total Equity		$72,000	
TOTAL LIABILITIES and OWNER'S EQUITY			$172,000

The Cash Flow Statement

The final statement is the cash flow statement. As the name suggests, this record tracks the flow of cash in and out of your business. A sample cash flow statement is shown in Exhibit 8-3.

Most financial consultants agree that cash flow projection is an essential planning tool for a growing business. We believe, because you're reading this book, you want your business to grow and prosper; therefore, we would recommend that you produce a cash flow statement each month to increase your odds of success.

Exhibit 8-3. A typical cash flow statement for a retail business.

Carol's Gift Emporium
Cash Flow Statement for December 2004

Beginning Cash Balance		$12,000
Cash Receipts (Sales)	$24,000	
Accounts Receivable Collection	1,200	
Total Cash Receipts		$25,200
Total Cash Available		$37,200
Cash Disbursements (Paid Out)		
Salaries	$8,000	
Payroll Expense	1,200	
Delivery Expense	1,800	
Supplies	1,200	
Rent	2,600	
Repairs and Maintenance	800	
Owner's Withdrawal	4,300	
Total Cash Disbursements		$19,900
Cash Flow		$5,300
Ending Cash Balance		$17,300

A Monthly Analysis

Many small businesses generate their financial statements at the end of the year. When tax time approaches they gather up their records and see how much they owe.

This is as dangerous to your business as driving your car seventy miles per hour down the freeway for twelve seconds with your eyes closed. Without monthly statements you are running blind in your business for twelve months.

When you only get management information once each year, you can only make corrections once each year. This presents a real challenge to effective financial management. Today's competition requires that you are aware of what's going on around you and are able to react quickly.

We recommend that you get all three financial statements at least once each month. This allows you to make adjustments (management decisions) every thirty days.

Many independent businesses find that once they are organized, and have their journals in place, the actual monthly summary only takes a short time to complete. You may feel that, even having the information, you still don't know more than you did before. Take heart, and don't give up.

In Chapter Nine, we'll give you some tools that will make using your financial statements much easier. You will see how to make adjustments in your business to slow the decline or accelerate improvements. The prerequisite to using the tools is having accurate and timely income statements, balance sheets, and cash flow statements.

Twelve Financial "Must Knows"

We've found that there are twelve pieces of financial information that are critical to success. Let us stress here that these twelve elements alone are not all you have to know to survive and prosper; they simply serve as a starting point.

These financial "must knows" are explained below. They will help you in thinking about critical elements of financial management. When you are comfortable with all twelve elements, you can move on to the more sophisticated management techniques and analysis tools.

The first five "must knows" come right off the income statement. They are: 1) Sales, 2) Cost of Goods Sold, 3) Gross Profit, 4) Operating Expenses, and 5) Net Income.

1. *Sales*. Sales, the first major item on your income statement, records the dollar volume of business your company has done over a period of time. This number reflects the level of exchange—usually money for products or services.

   Many businesses track this number daily, weekly, monthly, and yearly. The sales amount should be exclusive of sales tax collections and any returned merchandise. It can reflect the volume of services provided as well as products sold.

2. *Cost of Goods Sold*. The next major item on your income statement is the cost of goods sold, also commonly referred to as the cost of sales. This is not the amount of inventory you bought during the period, but rather the actual cost—including freight and handling—of the inventory that was sold. To obtain an accurate cost of goods sold, begin with an inventory level for the period. Add your purchases for the period to the beginning inventory to arrive at the total amount of goods available for sale. Subtract the ending inventory to get an accurate cost of goods sold. See Exhibit 8-4 for an example.

3. *Gross Profit*. The difference between sales and the cost of goods sold is Gross Profit. This "must know" tells you how much money is left from revenue to pay for operating expenses during the period.

4. *Operating Expenses*. The operating expenses, sometimes referred to as fixed expenses or overhead, are those incurred by being in business. These expenses are required to operate the business, regardless of the level of sales or activity. Operating expenses include the cost of such items as rent, insurance, administrative personnel, advertising, and supplies.

Exhibit 8-4. Calculating cost of goods sold.

Jack's House of Music
Cost of Goods Sold for December 2004

Beginning Inventory (November 30, 2004):	$112,400
Purchases Made in December 2004:	+76,600
Total Goods Available for Sale in December:	$189,000
Ending Inventory (December 31, 2004):	−110,000
Total Cost of Goods Sold (December, 2004)	$79,000

Every one of the new breed pays close attention to these expenses. Just as a high level of body fat is bad for an athlete, high operating expenses are unhealthy for small businesses.

5. *Net Income.* Net income is what's left of sales after all expenses—cost of goods sold and operating costs—are taken out. Net income is taxable income, not your take-home pay. This is a number that every business owner wants to increase.

6. *Inventory.* For most retail businesses, inventory plays an important role in financial management decisions. It's a "must know" number to manage. We pointed out earlier that you need monthly income statements, and that in order to have accurate cost of goods sold information, you need beginning and ending inventories for each month. This means that your cost of goods sold is only as accurate each month as your inventory count. Inventory control and monitoring may be the best reason to move into high technology.

There are two primary methods of monitoring inventory. The first is the periodic method, in which goods are physically counted periodically to establish the inventory level. The second method is the perpetual type, in which the inventory level is continuously maintained by adding in purchases when they occur and subtracting units as they are sold. The primary advantage of the perpetual method is that the current level of inventory is always known.

Exhibit 8-5 lists common inventory management goals. Exhibit 8-6 offers tips on eliminating obsolete inventory.

7. *Inventory Turnover.* This puzzle piece lets you know how fast your merchandise is moving. There are two methods that may be appropriate to use when determining this ratio. In method number 1—the stock-to-sales ratio—the average inventory is divided into net sales to determine the number of turns (average inventory is determined by taking the beginning inventory plus the ending inventory and dividing by 2).

In method number 2—the stock-to-cost-of-goods-sold ratio—the average inventory is divided into the cost of goods sold to determine the number of turns. To see how the numbers vary, look at the example in Exhibit 8-7:

Exhibit 8-5. Common inventory management goals.

Goals in managing inventory will vary from business to business. Here are some that apply to most businesses:

- When sales are *increasing*, grow your inventory at a slower percentage rate than sales.

- When sales are *decreasing*, reduce your inventory by a percentage greater than your sales decline.

- Decrease your inventory as a percentage of sales.

- Eliminate out-of-stock conditions.

- Decrease differences between actual counts and accounting records.

- Increase annual inventory turns.

Exhibit 8-6. Eliminating obsolete inventory.

Inventory can grow stale. Rather than sitting on it or throwing it away, try these tips:

1. *Trade it or barter with it.* Work with your suppliers to exchange your stale or dead inventory for other inventory that is salable. Some companies specialize in bartering inventories, and you may be able to trade with another business.

2. *Add value with it.* Package overstocked items with other goods to increase the value perception and close rate. An outdoor power equipment dealer packaged inexpensive grass trimmers with lawn mowers. "Buy the mower, get the trimmer free." This tactic helped him close lawn mower sales.

3. *Hold a special discount sale.* Any dollars recovered from stale inventory can be put back to work for you.

4. *Return it to the source.* Talk to your suppliers. If they won't give you a 100 percent return rate, try to negotiate whatever you can.

5. *Give it away.* Find a charity that will take your unwanted inventory and give you a tax deduction in return. Work the public relations angle too. The media may find your generosity newsworthy.

---

8. *Accounts Receivable Management.* Many small businesses extend unsecured credit to their customers as a method of boosting sales. We have worked with hundreds of "cash poor" businesses, and we often find that the reason for the lack of cash is poor accounts receivable management.

No one likes to tell customers no when they ask for additional credit or more time to pay. In addition, no one wants to be a hardnose and demand immediate payment even if the payment is past due. The result is often a significant drain on your cash flow as slow-paying customers use you as their bank

Exhibit 8-7. Two methods for determining inventory turnover.

Tennessee Valley Hardware

Sales	$1,000,000
Cost of Goods Sold	$750,000
Average Inventory	$125,000

Method one—Stock to Sales Ratio

$$\frac{\text{Sales}}{\text{Average Inventory}} = \text{turns} \qquad \frac{\$1,000,000}{\$125,000} = 8.0 \text{ turns}$$

Average Inventory	$125,000

Method two—Stock to Cost of Goods Sold Ratio

$$\frac{\text{Cost of Goods Sold}}{\text{Average Inventory}} = \text{turns} \qquad \frac{\$750,000}{\$125,000} = 6.0 \text{ turns}$$

Faster turnovers with either method are usually considered as positive. As a rule of thumb, shoot for six to seven turns until you get your industry's data. Then you may want to aim higher.

or credit card company. We suggest the following ten steps to manage your accounts receivable process.

1) Consider positioning yourself—as the new breed have—to accept all major credit cards. Then stick to a *cash, check, or credit cards only* policy.

2) If you decide to accept open accounts, establish a written credit policy and provide a copy to your customers.

3) Be selective in giving credit. You must have a method of determining who is creditworthy and who is not. Remem-

ber, not all customers who accept your credit terms will pay you.

4) Get a *signed* application from the customer that verifies that they understand your credit policies and agree to abide by them.

5) Do a credit check before you issue credit. Update each active credit file with a new credit report yearly.

6) Monitor your accounts receivable closely. An aging statement allows you to categorize your accounts as current (less than thirty days old), thirty to sixty days, sixty-one to ninety days, and over ninety days.

7) Make an effort to collect all accounts over thirty days old. Try a "second notice" billing, a personal letter, a phone call, or a personal visit. Don't let past due accounts grow older.

8) Build late-payment charges into your credit policy. Credit card companies charge for using money; banks do too—why shouldn't you?

9) To speed up your collectible period, bill more often. Instead of waiting until the end of the month to send out bills, send them out every other Friday.

10) Offer discounts for early payment if your margins will stand the decrease.

9. *Accounts Payable Management.* Frequently, accounts receivable problems are the root cause of accounts payable problems. If you aren't being paid for merchandise you've sold, it will be hard for you to pay your suppliers. Therefore, the best defense against payable problems is taking the offense in credit collections.

However, not all accounts payable problems are caused by slow-paying customers. Here is a list of other potential causes and solutions.

1. *Overly Aggressive Buying Practices.* Don't get carried away when you go to market. It's easy to buy more than you need, especially when attractive discount or payment terms are offered. The solution is to know your *open-to-buy numbers* and stick with them.

2. *Underestimating the Amount of Payables Due This Month.* The solution is to keep an accounts payable schedule so you can check one record to see what's due.

3. *Gradual Build-Up of Inventory.* Over time, building inventory can cause cash shortages. The solution is to monitor inventory levels closely and to slow buying levels to match sales.

4. *Inappropriate Use of Working Capital.* Don't put your short-term operating money into long-term assets. Arrange financing for fixed assets over an extended payback period.

Here are several advantages of accounts payable management:

1. You have improved relations with suppliers and manufacturers.

2. You are able to take advantage of discount terms offered for early payment.

3. You avoid interest and penalties added to late or partial payments.

4. Suppliers are often more willing to negotiate merchandise returns, discounts, terms, and trades with businesses who always pay on time.

5. Suppliers and manufacturers are more likely to offer *special deals* to their most creditworthy customers.

6. Your ability to borrow from your local lender is enhanced when you can demonstrate excellent trade credit history.

10. *Cash Position.* The cash position is a calculation of how much cash you must generate to pay typical monthly expenses. It is a method of working backwards from known expense levels to arrive at the level of daily sales required. Exhibit 8-8 shows a five-step method for calculating it for your business.

11. *Liability (Debt) Position.* The liability position of a business is a balance sheet check to determine whether the business is acquiring debt or paying it off. To determine your position, use the total assets of the business as your base value. For example, assume that Jones and Company's balance sheet shows $100,000 in total assets, $70,000 in total liabilities, and $30,000 in owner's equity. The amount of liabilities is 70 percent of total assets.

Generally speaking, we'd like to see this percentage trending downward. This would indicate that business assets are growing at a faster rate than debt or that the company is retiring debt as compared to assets.

We would recommend that you compare your percentage to your industry average. If your percentage is significantly higher than your industry's average, you may be overleveraged and need to reduce debt. If you are significantly below your industry's average, you may be underutilizing your assets and borrowing power.

12. *Owner's Equity Position.* The owner's equity position is the inverse of the liability position we discussed in number eleven. If the debt to assets percentage is 70 percent, as in the previous example, then the owner's equity position is 30 percent. If the debt percentage increases, the owner's equity decreases. If the business reduces debt, the ownership percentage increases.

Once again, there is no specific right or wrong ratio here, but generally we would prefer more ownership and less debt. A conservative, risk-averse owner would prefer high equity levels, where as a high-roller type wouldn't be concerned about more debt.

Exhibit 8-9 shows the ratios of some of the new breed. You'll

Exhibit 8-8. Calculating cash position.

1. Using last year's Income Statement, list the sales, gross profit, and operating expenses, as we've shown below.

Jones and Company

Sales 2004	$1,000,000
Gross Profit	250,000
Total Annual Operating Expenses	$ 200,000

2. Divide your sales by your gross profit.

    ($1,000,000 ÷ 250,000 = 4.0)

    This calculation reveals that you must produce $4 in sales to cover $1 in expenses. If your numbers come out to 2.71, it means you need $2.71 to cover $1 in expenses.

3. Determine the actual number of days your company is open for business. Our example, Jones and Company, closes on Sundays and six national holidays. It is open 307 days each year.

4. Divide your total annual operating expenses by the number of days you are open for business.

    ($200,000 ÷ 307 = $651.47)

    This tells us that Jones and Company's expenses average $651.47 for each day it is open for business.

5. We can now calculate the amount of cash sales and receivables collection—actual cash coming into your business—it will take to cover all expenses. Multiply your answer from Step 4 by the factor calculated in Step 2.

    ($651.47 x 4.0 = $2,605.88)

    We now know that Jones and Company must generate $2,605.88 in sales every day to generate enough gross profit to cover daily operating expenses. This figure represents the company's minimum cash position.

notice that these companies differ in the amount of leverage (debt to equity ratio) they are willing to accept.

Exhibit 8-9. Some new-breed, debt-to-equity ratios.

Company	Liability Position	Equity Position	Source Year
Wal-Mart	58%	42%	FY04
Target	65%	35%	FY04
Home Depot	35%	65%	FY04
Lowe's	46%	54%	FY04
Barnes and Noble	64%	36%	FY04
Best Buy	60%	40%	FY04
Circuit City	39%	61%	FY04
Toys "R" Us	59%	41%	FY04

Customer Information

Just as you can't manage numbers you don't have, it is difficult to serve customers you don't know. We aren't suggesting that your business can never satisfy needs and wants of customers unknown to you. Rather, we're saying that the better you know your customer, the more likely you are to anticipate their needs and wants and position your business to exceed their expectations.

While many small businesses struggle with the financial elements outlined earlier in this chapter, there is even a more barren wasteland that is devoid of facts and short of details. It is the land of *What do you know about the people who walk through your front door?*

Here are eighteen areas where you need specific customer information to compete with the megastores.

1) How many customers (potential buyers) walk through your front doors every day? every month? every year?

2) How many customers make purchases every day? every month? every year?

3) How much does your average customer spend with you each visit? each month? each year?

4) How would you define your customer using demographic characteristics (such as age, income, marital status, gender, household size, educational level, and employment)?

5) Identify three national or regional trends that affect your ability to serve customers in a *positive* manner.

6) Identify three trends that affect your business in a *negative* manner.

7) List five words your customers would use to describe your business image to others.

8) List ten specific benefits you offer your customers that Wal-Mart and other new-breed stores can't.

9) How many of the benefits you listed in answering question eight could your customers identify?

10) If your customers knew these benefits, how would they rank them in order of importance?

11) What are the ten most popular products or services your customers buy from you?

12) What percentage of your customers are repeat customers (regularly shop your trade area) as opposed to onetime shoppers (visitors, tourists)?

13) What percentage of your customers live within five miles of your store? ten miles? twenty-five miles?

14) What percentage of your customers do you know well enough to call by their full names? (Reading "Bob" on the patch of a mechanic's shirt doesn't count.)

15) What would your present customers like to buy from you that you aren't selling now?

16) What items do people leave your community to purchase most frequently? (This is known as "retail or service leakage.")

17) What hours would your customers like you to be open?

18) Could you create a mailing list of your top 100 customers? Top 200?

You will be able to use the customer information gathering tools in Chapter Nine to answer some of the questions above. Your goal should be to gather information from primary sources—via questionnaires, focus groups, and one-on-one interviews—and secondary sources— your own customer records, census data, trade publications, and other published information.

It is not imperative that you know everything today. However, you will need to start the process right away. Ignorance may be bliss, but in business, bliss can cause failure. Knowledge of your customers will help you serve them more effectively.

Productivity and Efficiency Information

In economics, productivity is defined as "being engaged in the creation of economic value." This concept is a critical component of successful small businesses: They all add value to the products and services they provide to their customers.

The efficiency factors are intertwined with value and productivity. Value is "perceived by the customer." It is the "balance of price versus quality and quantity." When we bring these factors together, they allow us to produce real value with minimal effort, expense, and waste.

This information becomes useful to you after you master some of the financial techniques and after you gather a significant amount of customer data. Your financial information is a prerequisite to good decision making, and customer information is a higher initial priority than productivity and efficiency factors.

However, once you move beyond the basic levels of information management, you'll find that you are spending more time on productivity and efficiency analysis and less time generating financial statements and customer data. As you improve your management skills and reach for greater efficiency and productivity, don't forget the basic premises presented earlier in this chapter. They are: You can't manage numbers you don't have, and you can't serve customers you don't know.

Managing productivity and efficiency (P&E) factors will use many components of information you are gathering now and will expand your need to gather and analyze additional data. For example, if you wish to determine how well your investment dollars are performing, you can use the return on investment tool in Chapter Nine. This ratio, or relationship, uses information from your income statement and balance sheet to quantify your return. This number can be compared to other businesses to see how efficiently you're using your money. In addition, you can compare your return to other forms of investment to see how productive your capital is.

Many P&E factors do not use financial statement or customer information. Instead, they require additional knowledge of your business operation. For example, a propane retailer may consider the number of gallons of propane delivered per truck as a measure of P&E. A photo processor may wish to consider the average rolls of film processed per employee per hour. An appliance dealer may wish to measure the closing effectiveness of the sales staff. These factors can be critical to business success, and you must make provisions for tracking information that may only be germane for your business or industry.

The final category of P&E information may use some information from traditional sources and other nontraditional sources. For example, a drugstore or hardware store may wish to measure sales volume per employee. They would combine sales information from the income statement (a traditional source) with payroll records (nontraditional). Or a clothing retailer may wish to monitor sales per square foot of selling space before and after redecorating. Once again, the analysis would require sales data (traditional) and facilities information from lease or real estate records or physical measurement (non-traditional).

There are three questions you should answer before gathering P&E information. They are:

1) Will having this information allow us to serve our customers more effectively?

2) Will having this information and sharing it with staff motivate them to be more productive and efficient?

3) Will this knowledge allow us to be more profitable or increase the value we pass on to our customer(s)?

Now you're ready to try some of the tools in the next chapter. We suggest that you read the entire chapter before trying to determine your next steps.

Key Points Checklist

☑ You can't manage numbers you don't have.

☑ You must have accurate, timely financial statements to make good decisions.

☑ Without monthly statements you are running blind in your business for twelve months.

☑ You will find several useful management tools in Chapter Nine.

The Manager's Tool Box

CHAPTER 9

*Man is a tool-using animal. Without tools he is nothing,
with tools he is all.*

—THOMAS CARLYLE

Tools save us countless hours and a lot of hard labor. In business, tools help us save time, and can also help us improve quality, increase accuracy, and guide us in good decision making.

Tools allow you to analyze financial statements to see what they can tell you about your business. Tools can help you find out what your customers really think about your products, services, and people. Tools can show if your business is operating efficiently. Tools can help you determine how strong your market position is, and whether or not you are vulnerable to the mega-merchants.

This chapter includes twenty-two management tools to help you evaluate various systems in your business, and determine the best actions to take when improvement is needed. A tool is just a tool until it is used properly. Read the instructions carefully to ensure that you are using each tool correctly.

We'll start with a short analysis we use to determine how a business is doing. We call it *The Thirty-Minute Checkup Tool*. This is not a sophisticated examination of your business. Rather, it is a quick check of your vital signs using company information and management's views to determine the health of your overall operation.

The Thirty-Minute Checkup Tool

It is easy in the stress of everyday management activities to lose touch with some fundamental success factors. This tool is designed to check some of the vital signs critical to the long-term success of your business. It will give you a feel for some of the areas where you may need more management attention, information, or effort.

To use this tool, make a copy from the book and answer the questions with a "Yes" or "No." Any question you don't know the answer to, mark as a "No."

General Business Operations

☐ Yes ☐ No   1) Are both sales and profits higher now than they were last year?

☐ Yes ☐ No   2) Are you making business improvements at a faster pace than your competition?

☐ Yes ☐ No   3) Are you providing any products or services today that you didn't a year ago?

☐ Yes ☐ No   4) Are you turning your inventory over at a higher rate than in previous years?

☐ Yes ☐ No   5) Are you delegating more tasks so you have more time to plan and manage long-term issues?

Marketing Issues

☐ Yes ☐ No   6) Can you list the ten customers who give you the most sales and profits?

☐ Yes ☐ No   7) Are you giving your customers better value than your competitors? (Are you sure?)

☐ Yes ☐ No   8) Are your promotion efforts bringing in new customers or clients every week?

☐ Yes ☐ No   9) Are your printed promotion tools (cards, brochures, letterhead, and so on) up-to-date and of high quality?

☐ Yes   ☐ No   10) Are all promotion efforts (advertising, publicity, and so on) aimed directly at your target customers?

Financial Issues

☐ Yes   ☐ No   11) Are your financial (accounting) records accurate, current, and well-organized?

☐ Yes   ☐ No   12) Do you get an accurate income statement and balance sheet to review each month?

☐ Yes   ☐ No   13) Do you own more of your business now than you did this time last year?

☐ Yes   ☐ No   14) Do you have a strong (solid and friendly) working relationship with your banker?

☐ Yes   ☐ No   15) Could you borrow more money tomorrow if you needed to capitalize on a great opportunity?

Human Resources

☐ Yes   ☐ No   16) Do your customers often compliment you on your good service and quality employees?

☐ Yes   ☐ No   17) Are you paying your employees as well as others in your area (salaries, benefits, and so on)?

☐ Yes   ☐ No   18) Are your employees usually positive and enthusiastic about their jobs?

☐ Yes   ☐ No   19) Have all of your employees received beneficial training in the past twelve months?

☐ Yes   ☐ No   20) Do you offer employees both cash and noncash incentives for work well done?

Technology Issues

☐ Yes   ☐ No   21) Have you learned at least one new software program in the past twelve months?

☐ Yes ☐ No 22) Can you list at least three areas where technology is improving your business efficiency?

☐ Yes ☐ No 23) Can you list two areas where technology might help you serve your customers better?

☐ Yes ☐ No 24) Are you at least "even" in the technology wars with your toughest competitors?

☐ Yes ☐ No 25) Does your current technology system give you the management information you need?

Now, add up your *yes* answers. If you scored:

- 23 to 25 *yes* answers: Your business sounds like it is in excellent health. Don't relax, but keep doing what you're doing.

- 18 to 22 *yes* answers: Overall you're doing pretty well. Look at any area with more than one "no" answer. You may want to make some improvements there.

- 13 to 17 *yes* answers: You have some management issues that need some concentrated attention. Any area with two or more no answers should receive your prompt attention.

- 12 or fewer *yes* answers: Your vital signs are weak. Quick, effective changes will be required to restore the health of the business.

The Common-Size Analysis Tool

A good way to analyze income statements and balance sheets is to use the common-size tool. Common-sizing is a technique that converts the dollar amounts on your financial statements to percentages. You use one element from the statement as a base value, and you compare all other elements to it.

Common-Sizing the Income Statement

The sales amount is the base value used in common-sizing the income statement. See Exhibit 9-1. All elements on the income statement are divided by sales to calculate common-sized percentages. For example, if the business generated $100,000 in sales for November, and the cost of goods sold was $68,000, the common-sized cost of goods sold would be 68 percent (68,000 ÷ 100,000). The advantage of this tool is that you can compare all income statement categories regardless of whether the business is growing or declining.

Notice in Exhibit 9-1 that all sales amounts, the base value, are 100 percent when common-sized. Divide any number on your income statement by the sales amount to get the common-size percentage.

Though all numbers change from year to year, we can see in 2003 that the cost of goods sold increased 5 percent compared to 2002. This jump is not obvious when looking at dollar amounts only, because sales also increased dramatically for the same period. Common-sizing

Exhibit 9-1. Common-sized income statements.

	2002	2003	2004
Sales	$100,000 (100%)	$111,500 (100%)	$98,000 (100%)
Cost of Goods Sold	$ 68,000 (68%)	$ 81,395 (73%)	$65,660 (67%)
Gross Profit	$ 32,000 (32%)	$ 30,105 (27%)	$32,340 (33%)
Operating Expenses	$ 22,000 (22%)	$ 25,645 (23%)	$22,540 (23%)
Net Income	$ 10,000 (10%)	$ 4,460 (4%)	$9,800 (10%)

allows you to see and correct the problem as the owner did in 2004. You can use this tool to isolate problem areas and make adjustments quickly.

Common-Sizing the Balance Sheet

The total assets amount is the base value used to common-size a balance sheet. See Exhibit 9-2. Total assets are always 100 percent, and every number on the balance sheet is compared to it. The common-size percentages are calculated by dividing the numbers by total assets.

Exhibit 9-2 shows three years of a simplified balance sheet reflecting a stable, growing company. The only apparent glitch was in 2003,

Exhibit 9-2. Common-sized balance sheets.

	2002	2003	2004
Current Assets	$ 30,000 (30%)	$ 33,000 (30%)	$ 34,000 (30%)
Fixed Assets	$ 70,000 (70%)	$ 77,000 (70%)	$ 80,000 (70%)
Total Assets	$100,000 (100%)	$110,000 (100%)	$114,000 (100%)
Current Liabilities	$ 15,000 (15%)	$ 19,800 (18%)	$ 17,000 (15%)
Long-term Liabilities	$ 50,000 (50%)	$ 48,000 (44%)	$ 46,000 (40%)
Owner's Equity	$ 35,000 (35%)	$ 42,200 (38%)	$ 51,000 (45%)
Total Liabilities and Equity	$100,000 (100%)	$110,000 (100%)	$114,000 (100%)

when current liabilities jumped 3 percent over the previous year. The owner spotted the jump through common-sizing and was able to bring the category back into line in 2004.

You may be curious about the jumps in owner's equity. Generally speaking, increases in the percentage of owner's equity—the amount of the business that is free of debt—are considered positive and desirable.

The Trend-Analysis Tool

Trend analysis is a financial management tool that uses information from the income statement, balance sheet, and cash flow statement. You use this tool to spread—layout side-by-side in columnar form—your numbers, and, by doing so, spot trends. For example, you might discover by spreading five years of income statements that while sales have increased every year, the gross margin has decreased both as a percentage of sales and in dollar volume. You can use a trend analysis to examine historical financial statements and to project future business conditions on the basis of historical trends. It works on both dollar volumes and common-sized percentages.

Using Trend Analysis on Income Statements

This tool can be used to compare day-to-day, week-to-week, month-to-month, and year-to-year trends. While all categories can be examined, usually only the major components of the income statement are spread initially.

For example, you may wish to examine income statements from the past five years. In examining sales, cost of goods sold, gross profit, operating expenses, and net income categories, you discover that your operating expenses are increasing both in dollar volume and as a percentage of sales. At that point, more detail is needed. You then need to spread every expense category (wages, payroll expense, insurance, supplies, repairs, vehicle expense, etc.) to determine the reason or reasons these expenses are growing disproportionately.

Using Trend Analysis on Balance Sheets and Cash Flow Statements

Balance sheets are most often compared on a year-to-year basis, though you can compare them as often as they are prepared. However, since significant changes occur at a more moderate pace on the balance sheet, it isn't as meaningful to do so. Using this tool on the cash flow statement is somewhat limited because usually cash flow statements are not common-sized. Therefore, you can only spread and trend dollar amounts. It can be used and is often effective in spotting and predicting cash flow trends, but other tools in this chapter may be more useful.

Ratio Analysis Tools

Ratios are comparisons of one number to another. We use ratios every day. We express the ratio of distance traveled compared to fuel used as miles per gallon. We discuss the cost of our home in relation to its size as dollars per square foot. These are useful, everyday ratios.

It seems natural that businesses use ratios to compare numbers as well. However, most independent businesses still aren't using ratios to help them compete with the mega-merchants.

There are nearly twenty common ratios used by various industries. We offer six as a starting point in this book.

Balance Sheet Ratios

These ratios measure liquidity, solvency, and leverage. Start with these three to see how your business is doing compared to your industry.

1. *Current Ratio.* This ratio measures your current assets compared to your current liabilities. This ratio answers the question: Does your business have enough current assets to pay off all of your current debts? Divide your total current assets by your total current liabilities to calculate this ratio.

$$\text{Current Ratio} = \frac{\text{Total Current Assets}}{\text{Total Current Liabilities}}$$

A larger ratio is preferred because it indicates your ability to pay all current bills with money to spare. The generally accepted standard is 2:1. Check with your trade association to find your industry's norms. A low ratio means that your business may not be able to pay all of its bills as quickly as it should. In addition, you may be missing out on cash discount terms and alienating suppliers. A high ratio means that you have a lot of cash that might be better off put to work in other areas of the business.

2. *Debt to Net Worth Ratio.* This ratio compares all of the liabilities (debt) of your business to the amount of the business you own. Divide total liabilities by your net worth.

$$\text{Debt to Worth Ratio} = \frac{\text{Total Liabilities}}{\text{Net Worth}}$$

Generally, the higher this ratio, the more risk your lender or creditors associate with your business. You gain increased flexibility as you lower this ratio.

A low ratio, such as 30 percent debt to 70 percent equity, means increased financial security and greater borrowing power. A high ratio, such as 60 percent or more of debt, indicates less financial security and limited ability to acquire outside funds.

Income Statement Ratios

There are two main ratios derived from the income statement. They are Gross Profit Margin ratio and the Net Income Margin ratio. Both of these ratios are critical to improving the amount of money generated on your bottom line.

1. *Gross Profit Margin Ratio.* This ratio is the percentage of sales left after subtracting the cost of goods sold from your sales. It indicates the percentage of sales available to pay operating expenses. Divide gross profit by net sales.

$$\text{Gross Profit Margin Ratio} = \frac{\text{Gross Profit}}{\text{Net Sales}}$$

Which is more desirable, a higher or lower margin? Interpretation of this number has grown significantly more complex with the advent of the new breed of discounters and category killers. For decades the typical retailer attempted to increase this ratio by keeping the cost of goods sold between 50 and 60 percent of sales. This left 40 to 50 percent as profit to pay operating expenses and generate income for the owner(s).

The new breed departed from this traditional approach and pushed gross profit margins below 20 percent of sales. By controlling operating expenses (overhead), these aggressive retailers were able to deliver profit to the shareholders and give their customers more value at the same time.

2. *Net Profit Margin Ratio.* Also referred to as the return on sales, this ratio is the percentage of sales dollars left after subtracting the cost of goods sold and all operating expenses except income taxes.

$$\text{Net Profit Margin Ratio} = \frac{\text{Net Profit Before Tax}}{\text{Net Sales}}$$

Ideally, this number would be as high as possible. This ratio measures the effectiveness of managing sales and expenses; in general, the higher the net income percentage (10 percent or more), the better.

A low ratio (5 percent or less) means that business expenses are too high *or that sales or profit margins are too low to support the overhead level.* A high ratio means that the business is earning well and that expenses are being controlled effectively.

Management Ratios

Some ratios require both income statement and balance sheet information to calculate. We refer to those ratios as management ratios.

1. *Inventory Turnover Ratio.* This ratio is an indication of how well you are managing your inventory. Generally, the more you turn your inventory, the more profit you generate. The two equations below reflect our mention in Chapter Eight that there are two methods of calculating this ratio. We suggest that you contact your industry trade association to see which method is more generally in use.

$$\text{Inventory Turnover Ratio} = \frac{\text{Net Sales}}{\text{Average Inventory (at Cost)}}$$

Alternate method:

$$\text{Inventory Turnover Ratio} = \frac{\text{Cost of Goods Sold}}{\text{Average Inventory (at Cost)}}$$

A low number of turns means that you may be overinventoried, or perhaps carrying too many slow-moving items. A high number of turns usually indicates effective use of inventory dollars and that your inventory is generally what your customers are looking for.

2. *Accounts Receivable Turnover Ratio.* This ratio measures how well you're collecting credit accounts. If you offer thirty-day credit terms, ideally you would collect your receivables twelve times per year.

$$\text{Accounts Receivable Turnover} = \frac{\text{Net Sales}}{\text{Accounts Receivable Balance}}$$

Generally, the more times you collect your receivables, the better. A low ratio (forty-five days or more) may mean you have a lax collection policy or have some slow-paying (potentially bad credit) accounts. A high turnover ratio (thirty days or less) may mean you have effective credit policies or that your accounts are all fast-paying.

Ratio-analysis tools can help you spot trends, compare your business operations to others in your industry, and establish goals to aim for. Ratios can be an early warning system for your business. No problem is more easily solved than a small one.

You may come to think of these ratio tools as your best friends. They are simple to use, easy to understand, and provide information you can't get effectively any other way.

These tools will never replace good management. However, if you use them, they can make you a better manager. You will have to be a better manager to stay ahead of your new breed of competitors.

The BackTrac Financial Troubleshooter Tool

All too often financial problems can be difficult to find and fix. Usually, the problem that we think we see is just a symptom of the problem, not the problem itself.

We have identified four common symptoms of troubled businesses. They are: (1) Low or declining net income, (2) Low or declining gross profit margin, (3) Low or declining sales level, and (4) Cash declines or shortages.

To use this tool (see Exhibit 9-3), first identify a symptom that is evident in your business, then backtrack from the symptom to find the potential causes. This will allow you to work on the potential problem, not the symptom.

The Promotion Spending Guide

One of the most frequently asked questions by small-business owners is, "How much should I spend on advertising and promotion?" Because we have never found a good source for an answer to this question, we created a generic tool to help you establish a starting point.

Caution: Please read the six caveats before using the guide.

1. Projecting a specific amount to spend on promotion is *not* an exact science. Because business types, sizes, and conditions vary so greatly, no tool such as the *Promotion Spending Guide* can predict the exact percentage of sales to be spent on promotion with

Exhibit 9-3. The BackTrac Financial Troubleshooter Tool.

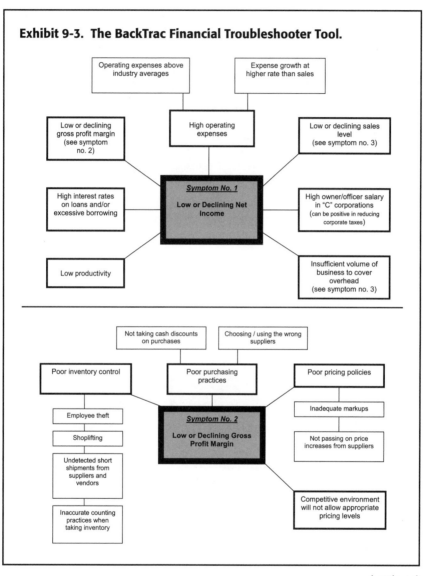

(continues)

Exhibit 9-3. (Continued.)

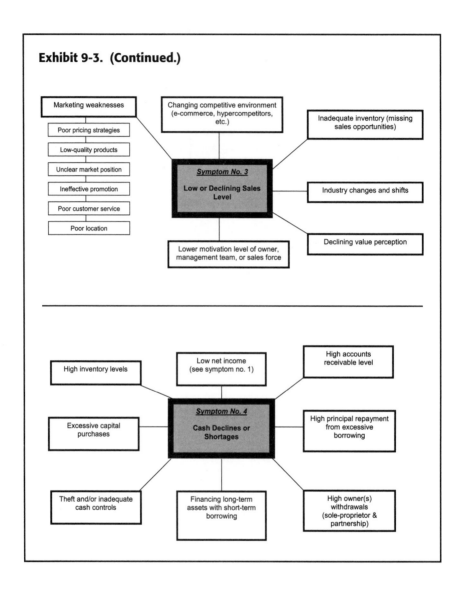

complete accuracy. It is only an aid, a guide to help you move in the right direction.

2. While we have attempted to factor in many variables in our questions, not all apply to all types of businesses, and we've probably missed some.

3. Because the cost of advertising varies so greatly between markets, some of you may be able to spend a lot less and still achieve great results, if your media costs are low. Others may be forced to spend significantly more to achieve similar success because of higher advertising costs.

4. If your spending level varies greatly from the guideline ranges—either higher or lower—you should adjust your spending in the proper direction . . . but move slowly. Don't try to take a big jump all in one year. If you increase spending greatly, you may not *see* positive results. If you reduce spending greatly, you may not *like* the results. Make incremental adjustments, and monitor the results closely.

5. Results may vary due to: your current profitability, amount and strength of your competition, the media costs in your trade area, the nature of your target customers, current pricing strategies, business location and access, past promotion success, and type of business.

6. No guarantee of success or improvement is expressed or implied. The user accepts full responsibility for all changes made while using this tool as a spending guide.

The Promotion Spending Guide

Answer each question by checking "yes" or "no." (If you don't know the answer, it's a "no.")

	Yes	No
1. Our sales are increasing each year.	☐	☐
2. Our profit is increasing each year.	☐	☐

	Yes	No
3. The number of walk-in customers is growing.	☐	☐
4. Everyone in our trade area knows we're here.	☐	☐
5. Everyone in our trade area knows what we sell.	☐	☐
6. Our location is very visible, and easy to find.	☐	☐
7. Our location has high "drive-by" traffic and lots of parking.	☐	☐
8. We've been in the same location for more than three years.	☐	☐
9. We have very little competition in our trade area.	☐	☐
10. Our competitor's prices are higher than ours.	☐	☐
11. Our advertising media costs are reasonable.	☐	☐
12. We use co-op advertising to lower promotion costs.	☐	☐
13. Our sales team (salesperson) is well trained.	☐	☐
14. Our inventory is very current. (No dead stock.)	☐	☐
15. We've added new lines or items this year.	☐	☐
16. We do a lot of "add-on" selling in our business.	☐	☐
17. All of our "name brands" are advertised nationally.	☐	☐
18. We have a current customer mailing list and use it often.	☐	☐
19. Our competitors all advertise less than we do.	☐	☐
20. We have taken customer surveys to see how they feel about us.	☐	☐
21. We get as much "walk-in" ("phone-in") traffic as we can handle.	☐	☐
22. We advertise regularly in more than one medium. (Newspaper, TV, radio, billboards, yellow pages, etc.)	☐	☐
23. We send our customers a regular newsletter with "news they can use."	☐	☐
24. We have a Web site, and update it at least monthly.	☐	☐
25. We cross-promote our Web site in other advertising.	☐	☐

Using the Guide:

1. Count the number of "no" answers.

Total "No" Answers ☐

2. Using the guideline ranges below, compare your current advertising "percent of sales" to the recommended amount. (To calcu-

late your current promotion expense as a percentage of sales, divide the total dollar amount spent on promotion by the total amount of sales. See example below.) If you are below the guideline ranges, you may need to increase your promotion budget.

Number of "No" Answers:	Your "Percentage of Sales Spent on Promotion" Target Is:
Less than 6	1 to 2 percent of sales
6 to 11	2 to 3 percent of sales
12 to 17	3 to 4 percent of sales
More than 17	5 to 6 percent of sales

Note of Caution: These are only guideline ranges. There are many factors to consider before you double or triple your advertising budget. Additional spending may not result in increased sales or larger profits. Don't overspend or be swayed by slick advertising sales folks. Remember that the reason we advertise is to get the right message, to the right people, at the right time.

Example: Calculating promotion costs as "percentage of sales."

Mickey's Art Supplies spent $5,400 last year on promotion. The company had total sales (revenues) of $200,000. To calculate the "percentage of sales" spent on promotion, divide $5,400 by $200,000. You should get .027, or 2.7 percent of sales.

The Thirty-Second Media Quiz Tool

This tool can accomplish two main objectives: First, to determine the media preferences of your customers, and second, to ascertain the effectiveness of your current promotion.

This brief survey can be used right in your business. We like to give the customer some incentive for filling it out. You can have them include their name and phone number and register them for a weekly gift certificate of $25.

Customer Survey

Please take a minute to answer the following questions. You will automatically be entered into our weekly drawing for a $25 gift certificate.

1. What newspapers do you read regularly?

	Daily	Sunday
1st choice	_____	_____
2nd choice	_____	_____

2. What radio stations do you listen to regularly?

	AM	FM
1st choice	_____	_____
2nd choice	_____	_____
3rd choice	_____	_____

3. Have you seen or heard any of our advertising recently? _____
_____

4. Do you remember where? _____

5. Name _____ Phone _____

Thanks for your help!

The Customer Satisfaction Survey Tool

If you want to know what your customers think about your business . . . ask them. Design some simple customer surveys and *ask* your customers to fill them out.

We'd like to know what you think about our service so we can serve you better.

1. Did you receive prompt, courteous service?   ☐ Yes   ☐ No

   Comments:

2. Was the individual who served you helpful and
   informative?   ☐ Yes   ☐ No

   Comments:

3. Were you satisfied with the selection you had to choose from?
       ☐ Yes   ☐ No

   Comments:

4. Were you satisfied with the product your purchased?   ☐ Yes   ☐ No

   Comments:

5. Would you do business with us again?   ☐ Yes   ☐ No

   Comments:

The Customer Batting Average Tool

This is one of our favorite tools because it helps you gather and analyze information that you can use to grow your business. To use this tool you must record three different numbers for the period you wish to analyze.

First, you must know your total customer traffic. This is an actual count of everyone who comes into your business or you make contact with.

The second number is the actual number of buyers. The third number is the amount of sales generated.

Using the information from Exhibit 9-4, we can calculate the Music

---

Exhibit 9-4. Sample form to track your customer batting average.

Customer Batting Average
The Music Mart—Week of September 11–16, 2004

Total Number of Walk-ins for Week	420
Total Number of Buyers (Transactions)	336
Total Sales for Week	$4,704
Customer Batting Average (Buyers ÷ Walk-ins)	.800
Average Dollars Per Sale (Sales ÷ buyers)	$14.00
Average Dollars Per Customer (Including Nonbuyers)	$11.20

Mart's customer batting average. Divide the number of buyers—336—by the total potential customers—420—to get .800, or a percentage of 80 percent. We now know that eight of ten people who walk through the front door purchase something. This number may be high or low depending on the industry and the season.

This tool also helps us develop other information. For example, we now know that the average customer who buys spends $14 (total sales divided by number of sales transactions). We also know that every customer who walks through the door is worth $11.20 in sales (total sales divided by total traffic).

We can use this information along with our customer profile to evaluate other parts of our business. Traffic counts can help evaluate the effectiveness of your advertising. The customer batting average can help evaluate the effectiveness of your sales staff or find weaknesses in your inventory levels. Most importantly, it gives everyone in your business something to shoot for. Your goal should be to improve all of these numbers.

Three Ways to Grow Your Business

There are three ways to improve your business using the information from the customer batting average tool.

1) *Increase walk-in traffic*—This can be accomplished with good promotion. Remember from the Music Mart example, each "walk-in" is worth $11.20 in sales.

2) *Increasing the customer batting average*—Turning walk-ins into buyers will involve several tactics. It is critical to discover why some customers didn't buy. Merchandising, pricing, customer service, personal selling, and inventory selection will provide the starting point.

3) *Increasing the amount of the average sale*—To succeed in this area, you will need to improve merchandising, suggestive (add-on) selling, product knowledge, and selling-up skills. It may also require adjustments in inventory selection and frequency of ordering.

All in all, this is a solid tool to help you learn more about your customers and to serve them better.

Variable Pricing System

The variable pricing system is a seven-step strategy for maintaining desired profit margins for your business without losing the perception of value in your customer's mind.

Step One—*Know your competitors' prices for any item you sell.* For example, let's assume you're selling a four-roll package of brand-name toilet tissue. A quick survey of the competition shows the same brand at Wal-Mart for 97 cents, Kmart at 99 cents, and a local supermarket at $1.49. Wal-Mart and Kmart have established your competitive target at under a dollar.

Your customers, who are not vitally interested in your success, take time to notice these prices. Since you are vitally interested, stay on your toes and make sure you know your competitors' prices.

Step Two—*Compare your prices to your competitors' prices.* In the example in step one, Wal-Mart is the price leader at 97 cents for the toilet tissue. If you're selling the same tissue at $1.29, your price is 32 cents higher, or a percentage difference of nearly 33 percent.

If you allow this price differential to go on, you may lose some perception of value. Your 33 percent higher price level may cause customers to believe you're higher on everything.

Compare prices often. Your customers are comparing every time they shop. We recommend a monthly general check in addition to reading weekly flyers and monitoring radio and television ads.

Step Three—*Determine price sensitivity.* Items that are sensitive to competitive pricing are known as *visible* items. Visible items include products and services that are utilized by a wide variety of customers, or items that are disposable or consumable, or are fast-moving. Visible items are frequently promoted and often used as *loss leaders* or *come-ons.* Most big-ticket items—cars, major appliances, furniture, and so on—will be price-shopped, and are therefore visible or price-sensitive.

In Exhibit 9-5, we provide a tool you can use to quickly determine a product's price sensitivity. We'll use the toilet tissue from the previous examples to do a sample sensitivity evaluation.

Step Four—*Know what overall gross profit margins you need to cover all costs.* Maintaining margin is a challenge for most businesses. In the sample income statement in Exhibit 9-6, we show a business that is operating with a gross profit margin of 40 percent. Stated another way, this business generates 40 cents on every dollar of sales to pay for all other costs.

It is important that you recognize all costs in determining the overall margin you need. In the above income statement, there are three types of cost. The first is *cost of goods sold;* the second is the *fixed or operating expenses;* and third is the *desired profit or net income.* For the purpose of this discussion, we include profit (net income) as a cost you must cover.

Your goal is to generate enough gross profit to cover your operating expenses and produce the net income percentage you desire. To follow through on Step Four, we need to maintain a gross profit of 40 percent in our example. Many businesses use a standard markup

Exhibit 9-5. Determining price sensitivity.

Brand Name: 4-roll package bathroom tissue

Characteristics:	YES	NO
• Used by a wide range of customers	☑	☐
• Disposable/consumable	☑	☐
• Fast-moving/high inventory turn	☑	☐
• Advertised and promoted heavily	☑	☐
• High-dollar-value item	☐	☑
• Limited selling season	☐	☑
• Frequently used as a "loss leader" Item	☑	☐
TOTAL (yes answers)	5	

Determination = Very Sensitive

Rating Scale—(Score 1 point for each yes answer.)

0 = not price-sensitive   1 = slightly sensitive
2 = somewhat sensitive   3 = moderately sensitive
4 = sensitive   5+ = very sensitive

Exhibit 9-6. Sample income statement.

Common-Sized Income Statement
(as a percentage of sales)

1) Sales	$100,000	100%
2) Cost of Goods Sold	− 60,000	− 60%
3) Gross Profit	40,000	40%
4) Operating Expenses	− 30,000	− 30%
5) Net Income Before Taxes	$ 10,000	10%

percentage to achieve their overall margin. In our simplified example, an item, which costs 60 cents, would sell for $1. Thirty cents would be used to pay for operating expenses, yielding 10 cents, or 10 percent net income.

This all sounds wonderfully simple until you realize that the chains are going to keep their prices very low on highly visible items. And, if you are going to keep your perception of value with your customers, you will have to break away from your old mark everything up 40 percent philosophy.

Your competitors know exactly what margins they want to maintain. One of the key benefits the new breed gets from the heavy investment they've made in technology is the ability to monitor daily margins. They can adjust the price mix immediately if margins start to slip. This is an important reason for you to have accurate financial statements every month.

Step Five—*Decrease margins on price-sensitive (visible) items that your competitors carry.* Your objective in this step is to lower your prices on visible items (price-sensitive) so that they are close to your competition . . . *even* if it means cutting them to near cost. (We'll show you how to get the margin back in Step Six.) We suggest that you bring your prices down to within 5–10 percent of the market leader's. You may even wish to advertise a few specials that are as low as your competitor's.

Note: You will not have to lower prices on all of your inventory, just the most price-sensitive items and those items that are exactly the same as your competitor's (such as same brand, same size, and same product number). For many retail stores the crossover items and price-sensitive items may only be 10 percent or less of the inventory count. However, even if it is 20 percent of your inventory on which you need to reduce prices, you still have the other 80 percent of your inventory on which to increase prices to get your profit margin back up.

Any discussion of lowering prices as a defense against low-price competition would be incomplete without the mention of price points. Certain "price points" are sensitive. For example, even though it means giving up 5 cents of profit, a price of 99 cents may generate significantly more sales and profit than a price of $1.04. Accordingly, a price of $9.99 seems to be much lower than a price of $10.49, even though it is only 50 cents less. Once you are in a range between price points, there seems to be little resistance to higher prices. For example, if an item is priced at $12.39, increasing the price to $12.99 appears to have little effect on sales volume.

Step Six—*Increase margins on items that are not price-sensitive (blind) items.* This is your opportunity to get back the margin you gave up on price-sensitive items in Step Five. Increase prices on all items that are not price-sensitive and items that are not carried by your competitors.

The main objective of Step Six is to equalize or improve the overall profit margin in your business. At the same time you are lowering prices in Step Five, you need to adjust prices on the *blind* items in this step.

The easiest way may be to simply increase your markup on all inventory that is not identified as price-sensitive. For example, assume that you reduced your overall profit margin to 37 percent when you lowered prices on your visible, crossover inventory. You will need to regain 3 percent to be even with where you were prior to reducing prices on price-sensitive items.

You may find that it will take an additional markup of 4 or 5 percent on your "blind" inventory to regain the 3 percent you gave up overall. Monitor this process closely to see what changes occur.

By using this technique, merchants often find that they can actually improve their gross profit margin while still keeping that all-important value perception.

Step Seven—*Continue the process.* To be a survivor you should continue using these steps from now on. You'll need to compare prices, monitor margins, and adjust pricing. The variable pricing system is an ongoing process, not a one-time, quick fix. You'll need to continually react to the marketplace. By keeping an eye on everyone's prices and monitoring your margins, you can position yourself to reap maximum profits.

One-Shot Productivity and Efficiency Tools

1. Sales per square foot. (Divide total net sales by the total number of square feet used by the business.)

2. Sales per square foot by department. (Divide total net sales for the department by the total number of square feet used by the department.)

3. Sales per employee. (Divide total net sales by the total number of employees. Add part-time employees together to get full-time equivalents—FTEs.)

4. Sales per hour. (Divide total net sales by total number of "open-for-business" hours.)

5. Gross profit per square foot. (Divide total gross profit by the total of square feet used by the business.

6. Gross profit per square foot by department. (Divide total gross profit earned by the department by the total number of square feet used by the department.)

7. Gross profit per employee. (Divide the total gross profit by the total number of employees—FTEs.)

8. Gross profit per hour. (Divide the total gross profit by the total number of hours you are open for business.)

9. Net income per square foot. (Divide total net income by the total number of square feet used by the business.)

10. Net income per employee. (Divide the total net income by the total number of employees—FTEs.)

11. Service revenue billed per service employee. (Divide total net service revenue by the total number of service employees—FTEs.)

12. Service hours billed per service employee. (Divide total service hours billed by the total number of service employees.)

Key Points Checklist

☑ Tools can help us to save time, allow us to save money, assist us in evaluating our business position, help us become more efficient, and assist us in making better decisions.

☑ Tools are of little value unless they are used in the manner intended.

☑ The tools in this chapter are designed to be used again and again. Make copies and compare recent results with past results. This application will help you spot areas for improvement.

Profiles of Success

CHAPTER 10

Success is a journey, not a destination.
—Ben Sweetland

The success profiles we have included in this chapter are the most interesting and diverse group of business owners we've ever interviewed. They include retailers, service companies, and manufacturers. These business owners are some of the best of their various industries.

They are all thriving where big-boxes and big corporations dominate. They are achieving double- and in some cases even triple-digit growth, improving their bottom lines, and building wealth in their businesses.

Barry Steinberg, Bill Hanson, Jr., Jim and Roger Myers, Carl Reineke, Chris and Tracy White, and Alex Giftos have opened additional locations to capture greater market share.

Aledia Hunt Tush, Jerrold Taylor, and Gary Sage have expanded their single-location operations to allow for increased inventory, sales, and production. Berlin G. Myers, Jr., Don Griffin, Chris Campbell, Bill Marshall, and Ken Dumminger have focused on updating their existing facilities and maximizing their return on investment.

There is no cookie-cutter approach to their success. Each entrepreneur is different, and so are the businesses they run. What they have in common is that they are using the techniques we've detailed throughout this book to successfully take on the big-boxes and mega-competitors. They work hard, work smart, and are quick to implement changes that give them a distinctive competitive advantage.

They are focused on results, obsessed with quality, and concentrate on building relationships. They are growing sales, cultivating customer relationships, and most importantly multiplying profit.

The important thing for you the reader to remember is that these are *ordinary* people who are achieving *extraordinary* results. They are doing the right things, and they are doing them well. You can too!

In Boston, It's the Service, Not the Beans

For independent retailer Barry Steinberg, owner of Direct Tire and Auto Service in Watertown, Massachusetts, there is only one way to stand out in a marketplace where brand-name competitors saturate every corner. That way is *service*. When Wal-Mart, Sam's, Sears, NTB, and Town Fair Tire began to slash prices to lure customers, Steinberg refused to play the "who can sell it for less" game.

"The best competitive move I ever made was deciding not to compete on price," Steinberg says. "We know all customers want value, so we give them more for their money by providing top-quality products and service that no discounters can match."

Steinberg's strategy is working. He now has four locations, racks up annual sales in excess of $14 million, and employs eighty-six people who are paid well above the prevailing wage rate in the area. He has been named The Modern Tire Dealer of the Year, received the prestigious President's Award from the New England Tire and Service Association, and was recently honored as the Retailer of the Year by the Retail Association of Massachusetts.

Steinberg's retail and service success and well-deserved accolades can be traced to taking care of the customer. "Our service is what we are known for in the Boston area," he says. "We take care of our customers like they were our own grandparents."

More importantly, Steinberg gives his customers something more valuable than money. He gives them *time*. At the discounters, it may take a half-day or more just to buy tires and have them installed. All this time you're waiting in the stuffy, not-so-clean waiting room with stale coffee, and chairs that were provided by the lowest bidder.

It never happens that way at Direct Tire and Auto Service. Rather than wait around, you can pick up one of the free loaner cars and be on your way. You can go on to the office, home, or shopping. Your time is your own. Of course, if you choose to wait, the waiting room is spotless, and there is free gourmet coffee, soft drinks, herbal teas, and fresh pastries from the bakery across the street.

Regarding the free loaner car concept, everyone loves it except Steinberg's accountant. "My accountant looks at the 'loaner car expense' and thinks I'm nuts," Steinberg laughs. Then, being serious, he adds, "But we're not here for my accountant, we're here to take care of our customers. They love the flexibility and time savings of the loaner cars, so we'll keep them."

Steinberg is more than just a successful business owner, nationally recognized retailer, and innovative entrepreneur. He and his wife, Penny, care deeply about giving back to their community. They work hard on charitable projects that are bringing a brighter future to the area. Next year, the thirtieth anniversary of Direct Tire and Auto Service, Steinberg has a goal to raise $100,000 through joint promotions with the local media for local Boston charities.

The Steinberg formula: Take good care of customers and employees, do the right things well, and give back to your community. We couldn't say it any better.

Magnolias, Spanish Moss, and the Cleanest Lumberyard in America

In a sleepy little town in South Carolina, you wouldn't expect to find one of the best-run, family-owned businesses in the country. But that is exactly what you'll find at 350 North Main in Summerville, South Carolina, the home of Berlin G. Myers Lumber, Corp. (BMLC).

Amid the magnolias, moss-covered pines, and the easy pace of southern living, beats the heart of a giant killer. BMLC is thriving in one of the toughest industries in retail. Berlin G. Myers, Jr., says, "We're thriving because of the competition. Our sales have doubled since all the big-boxes came into the area."

The building-materials industry boasts the number two retailer in the world, Home Depot, and the number twelve chain, Lowes. Throw in a few thousand Ace Hardwares, True Values, HWIs, and local independents, and you've got a competitor's nightmare.

But Myers, Jr., hasn't lost any sleep. Instead, BMLC has concentrated all of their efforts into refining what they do best. What they do best includes supplying only the highest-quality building materials, ensuring that every customer is waited on and cared for personally, and spending time on the floor with customers every day. "You can't run this kind of business from the back room," he says. "Our customers are our friends. They like to see us, and we sure like to see them. It's a great way for us to know what they are thinking."

Myers, Jr., likes to point out the value his customers receive by buying the best. "For example, our price may be 5 percent higher on a complete package of lumber to build a home," he says. "However, it's not uncommon for cheaper grades of lumber from the big-boxes to have a waste factor of 10 percent. That is, boards that are bowed beyond use, too full of knots to support a load, and often split as well. When you factor in the time a contractor has to spend sorting through the piles for a good straight board to frame a door or window, quality lumber may actually save as much as 5 to 8 percent."

Employees also play a major role in the Myerses' success. Myers, Jr., says, "We could not run this business without our employees. We've got good people whom we can trust to provide honest answers to questions, gather good feedback, and support each other." BLMCs 35 employees not only take good care of customers, they provide valuable feedback on the competition as well.

If you visit the beautiful state of South Carolina, take a trip back into time and visit some of the antebellum homes, stop by the Magnolia Plantation and Gardens (between Charleston and Summerville), or just spend a little time at the beach. Oh yes, don't forget to see the cleanest lumberyard in America at 350 North Main in Summerville.

Where the Pros Shop and Play

Kid Rock, The Eagles, the late Ronald Reagan, Stevie Wonder, Donny Osmond, Neal Diamond, and the late Ray Charles. What do these people have in common? They were, or are currently, customers of West L.A. Music in Los Angeles.

"We've served many of the world's top entertainers," says owner Don Griffin. "We're proud of our customer list, and we mean it when we say this is where the pros shop."

Recently, Stevie Wonder came in the store to try out some of the newest microphones. "He sat down at a piano, and we set up mikes for him to try," says Griffin. "What a thrill that was for our other customers!"

While celebrities and music stars make frequent appearances at West L.A. Music, Griffin is quick to point out that the business exists to serve all customers, rich or poor, famous or not. "We're here for one reason: to serve the customer. When you walk in our front door, you become a celebrity to us. We know our success is tied to building lasting relationships with every customer."

Griffin has several words of encouragement for other small-business owners. "I couldn't run this business without great employees," he says. "We hire the best people we can find, train them well, and provide incentives to keep them motivated." In addition to financial incentives, Griffin uses recognition, awards, and special outings. "We may take our top performers to a ballgame or a special event," he says.

Griffin also believes in continuing education. "We must continue to build our personal skills and knowledge base in order to grow and prosper," he says. "We are fortunate in the music industry to have a trade association that excels in education." Although Griffin holds a master's degree in business from UCLA, he and his employees regularly attend training sessions at the International Music Products Association conventions.

"Our best competitive strategy is to stay current with technology changes in the music business," he says. "Our power niche is to be at the forefront of music innovation. Our professional customers are savvy. They want the latest technology as soon as it's available. Occasionally, they will bring us information on a new product or line that the manufacturers haven't even told us about yet."

Recently, West L.A. Music installed a complete recording studio in

Kid Rock's new bus. Now the superstar can create on the road, while traveling between appearances. That's the kind of innovation Griffin has built his business on.

Griffin also utilizes a buying group to help him achieve an exclusive product mix and better pricing. "There are only two ways to improve profits," he says. "You can increase revenues or decrease costs."

Another key for Griffin's success is integrity. "We demand 100 percent integrity and honesty from everyone who works here," he says. "We never cut any corners, never work in the gray areas, and never compromise our integrity with our customers."

Griffin also believes in giving back to the community. "Over the years, we've donated hundreds of autographed guitars to local charities," he says. "An autograph from a music superstar can turn an average guitar into an auction piece that can bring thousands."

For Griffin, the past decade has been one of solid growth in revenues and income. Griffin sums up the experience: "Despite pressure from the competition, and customers who expect more for less, this business is still fun."

Sun, Saltwater, and Success

Siesta Key. Sounds like a quiet vacation hideaway where you can relax, catch some rays, and watch the world go by. And it is that. But Siesta Key is also a hotbed of entrepreneurial activity and home to another unique "profile of success" business owner.

Aledia Hunt Tush owns and operates CB's Saltwater Outfitters, known simply as Mr. CB's. Mr. CB's is not your average bait and tackle shop, or beachwear boutique, or boat rental place.

Mr. CB's does do all of those things, but the core success of the business is based on providing customers memorable experiences in, around, or on the water.

Siesta Key is a waterfront community near Sarasota, Florida. Tourists typically provide 50 to 60 percent of Mr. CB's annual business, but the locals have also discovered that if you are looking for fun, fish, and the freedom of the open water, Mr. CB's is the place to go.

Despite downturns in past economies, and the fickle nature of the tourism industry, Mr. CB's has maintained consistent growth over the years. "We've added new products and product lines," Tush says. "We've revamped and remodeled, and added a lot of space and convenience for our customers."

One of the key services Mr. CB's provides is local information. "We rely on our in-house experts," Tush says. "No one knows current fishing conditions and local hot spots as well as those who are out on the water every day. Our captains and guides are wonderful; they'll talk to anyone who's interested.

"They know where the fish are, and what tackle is working," she says. For the customer this translates into catching trophy fish as opposed to drowning worms.

While Tush is a retailer, it's the service side of the business that's helped her battle the discounters. "Wal-Mart can't rent you a boat, sell you live bait, repair your rod and reel, or tell you where the fish are," she says. "But we can."

Mr. CB's provides regular seminars to educate fishermen about night fishing, specialty fishing,—you can learn how to catch a snook— and a host of other topics. They do ladies clinics and cosponsor a community-wide event called "Ladies, let's go fishing."

Tush is a great example of what a hardworking business owner can accomplish. "We're open 7 A.M. to 6 P.M. every day but Christmas," she says. Her efforts and hard work are succeeding. Recently Tush was named the Sarasota Chamber of Commerce's "Woman Entrepreneur of the Year." The Florida Retail Federation honored her as the "Top Retailer of the Year" in her size division, and she was named "Conservationist of the Year" by the Sarasota Chapter of the Coastal Conservation Association.

Hard word, smart work, great employees, and a customer-centered focus sounds like a formula for success. And for Aledia Hunt Tush, it is.

Sawing Out a Chunk of Market Share

The computerized industrial saw industry is a cutthroat, dog-eat-dog environment. The Goliath of the industry is a part of Warren Buffett's empire. Enough said.

However, where you find giants, you'll always find Davids. Monet De Sauw of Fulton, Missouri, is just such a competitor. Lacking the billions of dollars that are behind their major competitors, the three owners quietly set about cutting out a chunk of market share. They are succeeding.

In 1998, Jerrold Taylor, Jack Schulz, and Kevin Troesser purchased Monet De Sauw from its retiring owner. As they looked closely at the company and product line they had purchased, all they could see was positive potential. "What we found was solid, but aging engineering, good overall design, and a firm foundation to work from," Taylor says.

The first step for the new owners was to visit existing customers. They asked what users thought about the product. What were its strengths? What needed fixing? How could it be improved? The result was a better product line that reflected customers' needs and wants.

Monet De Sauw focused first on underserved customers: smaller companies whose remote locations meant that the bigger manufacturers weren't serving them. The customer liked what they saw and began to buy.

"In six short years, we've grown from dead last among the big four in the industry to number two in terms of units sold," says Taylor. "We know we give our customers the best value in the saw industry. It's value they can see: We overdesign our new saws, and even take their old saws in trade."

Taylor explains how the company builds in value. "We buy right, we keep our overhead costs below industry averages, and pass part of that savings right on to the customer," Taylor says. "We've streamlined our manufacturing process, so we can produce a custom saw in just eight weeks."

Sales have grown at near triple-digit rates for the past six years. "We are now five times as large—saleswise—as we were six years ago," Taylor stresses. "You know you're doing something right when customers respond like that." Taylor credits the growth to an aggressive marketing campaign. "Early on, we spent nearly 10 percent of our gross revenue in trade publications, on trade shows, direct mailings, and personal visits," he says. "We've found that when you back your marketing with quality products and great service, the consistent identification brings product recognition that leads to sales."

Taylor says that in a nutshell, Monet De Sauw's success comes from four basic focus areas. "Surround yourself with quality people, think smart and work accordingly, offer a quality product, and involve your customers in every aspect of your business," Taylor advises.

"We have a little slogan we like," Taylor said. "When better saws are built, De Sauw will build them." In a few months, Monet De Sauw will introduce a brand-new saw. The management team turned to a customer for design guidance. "We went to one of the sharpest customers in the industry for input," Taylor says. "Together we've designed a saw that will meet the needs of thousands of customers." The first saw will be placed in the partnering customer's main production plant for beta testing.

Monet De Sauw has used their success formula to cut out some serious market share. Which proves that whether you are in retail, service, or manufacturing—it's still all about doing the right things well.

A Time to Refocus in the Big Apple

For Bill Hanson, Jr., owner of Reliable Office Systems, Inc., it was time to refocus. His father, Bill Hanson, Sr., had seen the office supply crash coming in the early 1990s. The big-boxes were chewing away at market share, and margins were disappearing faster than biscuits in a boarding house.

When Hanson, Sr., retired, Hanson, Jr., inherited the reins. He knew the industry, but wanted to stay away from the commodity price wars. So when he evaluated the New York markets he planned to serve, he found that the business equipment side offered the best opportunities.

Hanson believes that the technology he sells can help other small-business owners stay ahead of their own competition. "We can help our customers save time and money," he says proudly. "In addition, we can show them how to be more productive, improve their business image, and be more efficient at the same time."

During the past three years, Hanson has seen steady revenue increases of 15 percent or more per year. He attributes this sales success to having top-notch people. "I couldn't run this business without quality technicians and a solid sales staff," he says. "Our salespeople find new customers every day, and the quality of our service helps us build relationships that will last. Satisfied customers are everything to this business."

"We are known for our service," he says. "Whether in Manhattan or on Staten Island, we provide quality service, quick response time, and a real person on the phone to deal with."

Hanson's efforts in caring for customers and going beyond just meeting their needs is bringing Reliable Office Systems, Inc., industry recognition. Recently the company received the coveted Canon Outstanding Partner Award. "It doesn't get much better than that," Hanson says. "It's a goal every dealer strives for. Going with Canon was the best competitive move we ever made."

When Hanson needs advice, he still turns to his father who founded the business in 1975. He also consults with his trade association. "You can always use an outside source to learn about the trends that are happening in your industry," he says. "But you also have to stay close to your own business."

Hanson is a CPA, and staying on top of his management information system is a high priority. "We know what's going on at all times financially," he says. "Nearly every decision we make affects our financials."

Hanson points out one way that Reliable sets itself apart from its competitors. "We aren't the biggest business machines company, but we are better," Hanson says. "Our competitors are becoming wary of our efforts. They know that if we continue to get better, we will grow bigger. And they know that our growth will very likely come at their expense."

Hanson believes in giving back to the communities they serve. "We're active in service clubs, and support many charitable organizations. We provide equipment at cost to nonprofits, and often donate equipment to area schools. It's a joy to give back," Hanson admits. "There's real satisfaction in knowing you can help."

Local Pharmacist Bests National Players

Jim and Roger Myers have achieved nearly 20 percent growth every year for the past five years. That is how they have handled strong competition from every national chain in their market.

The Tuscaloosa, Alabama–based chain Jim Myers Drugs, Inc., has grown from two small stores in 1994, to five stores today. In addition to double-digit sales growth, Myers stores rack up impressive sales that are more than double the square foot sales of all major chains.

"We've worked hard at this business," says Jim Myers. "We work hard for our customers. They've rewarded us with their business and their loyalty." Many of Myers's customers have done business with him since he started the business thirty years ago.

For Myers, taking care of customers is the number one priority of the business. "We carry a lot of inventory that Wal-Mart and the other chains don't bother with," he says. "The result is that we can fill most prescriptions on the first visit. When you are sick and don't feel well anyway, getting what you need immediately is a real advantage." Myers says his typical first visit–fill rate for prescriptions is more than 98 percent. "That's a real-time savings and convenience for our customers," he adds.

Myers also delivers. "We keep seventeen delivery vehicles busy with home deliveries of prescriptions and durable medical equipment and supplies," he says. "This is another way we add value for our customers." Jim Myers Drug also offers other services, such as free screening for glucose and blood pressure, and free seminars to help customers stay informed of the latest treatment options and techniques.

Myers says his best competitive decision was moving his main store to a better location some years ago. "Though we only moved two blocks, we increased our store size by six times," he says. "We added more than fifty parking spaces. The customers loved it, and we sure needed the space."

Myers gets key management information every month, and uses technology to stay current on the stores' financial performance. He recently installed a robot for dispensing capsules and tablet prescriptions. "We wanted both accuracy and speed," he says. "Customers are happy because they can get in and out more quickly."

Myers also believes in the team concept. "We treat our employees and our customers like they are part of our family," he says. "We work hard to include every employee and make them feel like they are part of the business."

The Myers have made many revisions to their stores over the years. "We've managed to keep an open mind about change," Jim Myers admits. "We try to be consistent in policy, but we have to constantly make changes in order to improve."

Myers participates in a cooperative buying group that helps keep the competitive edge sharp. "We are able to improve our pricing structure, lower our advertising costs, and stay up with industry trends," he says. "When you're independent, you need every advantage you can get."

Jim Myers Drug, Inc., is also an active community supporter. "We've always recognized our responsibility to our community," Myers says. "We're involved in our churches, the Chamber of Commerce, the University of Alabama, the United Way, the local hospice, and dozens of other worthwhile causes."

Myers has a prescription for success: Treat customers and employees like family, know your business and your industry, give back to your community, and be willing to make changes. Not only do these principles follow the best practices of great competitors, they also demonstrate a profile of success.

Just Do What You Say You Are Going to Do

Hoover, Alabama, is a fast-growth area near Birmingham. It is also home to a four-year-old independent rental business that keeps managing partner Chris Campbell excited about going to work. "From the time I worked in a rental store as a kid, I've wanted to be in the rental business," he says. "I love coming to work every day."

Campbell has two partners who helped establish Alabama Rentals, which Campbell operates on a day-to-day basis. "We've averaged nearly 15 percent in annual growth every year," Campbell says. "We are getting stronger and more competitive, and as long as we stay focused on getting better, we'll continue to grow."

Nearly every national chain in the rental industry surrounds Alabama Rentals. "Our main job is to stand out from the pack," Campbell says.

Campbell's strategy contains four main components. First and foremost is service. "The best way we can distance ourselves from the national chains is the high level of service we're committed to," he says. "And we even look at service in a different way than the chains do."

For Campbell, service begins with the *product*. "We start by making certain every product we rent is ready to go. Every rental item must have a "green tag" on it before it can be rented out," he says. "We do a thorough inspection and check every fluid level, maintenance item, and operational feature. We have one specialist who preps the large equipment such as bobcats, backhoes, and dozers, and another who handles all the smaller equipment.

"Our service continues when we get a call from a customer and we promise a delivery time," Campbell says. "We make certain we arrive on time. That's our policy, and we stick to it. We make on-time deliveries, we don't make excuses.

"Our goal with our service is to create a lifetime customer," he adds. "Our salespeople are taught to build relationships before they try to sell anything."

The second strategy Alabama Rentals employs is to use systems to manage the business with. "We use technology to do our financial analysis, find inventory weaknesses, and track customer patterns," Campbell says. "I couldn't run this business effectively without my computer and the systems we've created."

Another success focus area for Campbell is integrity. "We know our competitors make promises every day they can't keep. That's not our way," he says. "We're committed to doing exactly what we say we'll do, every time. Once the customer has experienced that, they develop a level of trust in you and your business."

The final area where Alabama Rentals excels is in the area of marketing. "The best competitive move we ever made was to develop a professional logo to establish our company as a bona fide player in the rental industry," Campbell says. "We use the logo on every truck, piece of equipment, sign, uniform, piece of paperwork, and promotion. There's never any doubt in the customer's mind that this equipment, delivery, driver, or mechanic is from Alabama Rentals."

Campbell thrives on the variety the business brings. "It's never dull around here; there is always a new challenge," he says. "We've got the best people in the area working for us, and they enjoy the challenges as well. We pay above the average wage rate, and we expect a lot from our folks, and they deliver."

Recently, Campbell was elected as a vice president for the American Rental Association. Of this honor he simply says, "I'm looking forward to serving, and I know I'll learn a lot. In this business, learning is important."

You Can Paint Your Own Niche

In the heart of St. Louis's most affluent western suburbs is where you will find all three Reineke Decorating Centers. Owner Carl Reineke located his stores there for a reason. "We found our niche," he says. "This is where our target customers are, and we're here for their convenience."

Reineke serves two distinctively different customer bases from his stores. "Our retail customers are typically women, 30 to 50 in age, with household incomes of $75,000 and up," he says. "They are well-educated, well-read, and generally know what they are looking for."

The second customer base his stores serve is the smaller, high-end contractor. These are usually one- or two-man shops that work exclusively in the more affluent communities. They do the highest quality work and demand the best materials available.

"We've learned to become niche marketers," Reineke says. "We know that both of our main customer groups care more about how the work looks when finished than whether they saved three dollars on the paint."

Reineke has an abundance of low-price competitors ranging from all the usual big-boxes to company-owned paint stores. "They caused us to rethink our position," he says. "Instead of trying to drive sales and compete on price, we're focused on providing the highest-quality products, unmatchable levels of service, and building our bottom line. Profit keeps you in business, and you generate it when your customers can see the value and benefits of what you are offering them."

Reineke has strengthened his store positions through better purchasing and inventory management. "Technology has helped us become better managers in these areas," he readily admits. "We are improving our inventory turns, and are deeper in the lines that are producing for us. In addition, we've been able to maintain wide selections so that most special requests can be satisfied right on the spot."

Another key success strategy for Reineke is to surround himself with bright, articulate people. "We hire only the best," he says. "I can't be in all three stores all the time, so we need competent people in every position from sales to mixing." Reineke lets his managers manage. "They know that retail is in the details. They know what to do, and we let them do it," he says.

Reineke points out how his staff adds value to every customer purchase. "We know our products," he says. "We help our customers select the best product for their need, find the right finish, and the perfect color—even if we have to customize it. All of our people are trained to do this."

Reineke belongs to a buying group that helps him keep control of costs and also helps him stay informed. "We've developed a strong camaraderie with other group members," he says. "We all face common problems, and everyone is willing to share what's working for them." He has also served as president of the Paint and Decorators Retail Association.

Reineke sums up his twenty-nine years in business this way, "This is a family-owned business," he stresses. "My wife, Pam, and our children have contributed greatly to its success. We're still having fun, but today's customers are more challenging than ever before. We have to work a lot harder to please them and win their loyalty. But that is still our goal, and it's why we grow."

A Trip to the White House . . . in Wisconsin

Wait! Before you challenge our geographic integrity, we aren't talking about *that* White House. We're talking about the White House of Music stores located in Waukesha, Watertown, and West Bend, Wisconsin.

Owners Chris and Tracy White have taken a page right out of the Wal-Mart book and surrounded the Milwaukee metropolitan area with three unique and exciting music stores. The Milwaukee metro area boasts more than a million consumers, and the majority are within minutes of a White House of Music location.

The Whites have consistently increased sales every year, and have held profits steady despite intense big-box competition and low-quality foreign imports. It's quite a challenge, but Chris White says, "I'm having more fun running the stores than ever before."

The key elements of the Whites' success include building lifetime customer relationships, controlling costs, continual improvement, and getting timely management information. Chris White explained his philosophy on winning lifetime customers. "People like doing business with people they know . . . our job is to get to know every customer. Once we're acquainted, we strive to earn their trust and keep it. Customer loyalty is still very attainable, but you can't earn loyalty by cutting prices."

One of the ways the Whites focus on relationship building is through their professional sales force. No, these are not high-powered, high-pressure professionals, they are normal folks who have been trained to educate first, and then help the customers reach buying decisions that are best for them. "We're really educators," White said. "We teach about music, instruments, life, and fun. We want to get people involved in music so they can enjoy life to the fullest. Music is relaxing and fulfilling, and it's a great stress eliminator."

White also believes that one of his competitive advantages is tied to controlling costs. "I think Benjamin Franklin said, 'A penny saved is a penny earned.' I like to save dollars," White says. He monitors his income statements closely, and belongs to a buying group that not only helps him reduce his cost of goods sold, but also gives him access to proprietary brands and products the mass merchandisers can't buy.

Continual improvement is more than just a catch phrase at White House of Music. White sums it up this way, "To be competitive, we must be better today than we were yesterday. To stay competitive, we must be better tomorrow than we are today."

White keeps his competitive edge sharp by being active in the music industry. As a twenty-nine-year-old, he served as the president of the National Association of Young Music Merchants and was a member of the Board of Directors for the International Music Products Association. This trade association's university has an international reputation for providing some of the best retail training programs in the world.

Another strength at the White House of Music stores is getting timely management information. White says, "Financial information is critical to every aspect of our business. It never seems to come soon enough, even though we get it quickly."

An Employee-Owned Bank—Not an Aesop Fable

Nestled in the hills of the Missouri Ozarks, adjacent to the Mark Twain National Forest, and only miles from the population center of the United States, there is a little bank that is unlike any other. It is owned by its janitor . . . and the tellers . . . and the vice presidents . . . and the receptionists. In fact, Phelps County Bank is 100 percent owned by its employees.

The unique little bank is located at 718 North Pine Street in Rolla, Missouri, and also has a branch in St. James. It is organized under an Employee Stock Ownership Program.

Bill Marshall, whose business card calls out his title as "owner"—as do those of *every employee*—serves as president of the bank. He spoke to us regarding the value of having every employee as a vested owner. "We've found that great employees create great customers. They know that their success is directly related to how well they take care of customers, so they work hard to attract the best."

One of the largest banking chains in the world—Bank of America—is about 100 feet down the street. How can a little home-owned bank compete with the thousands of services available through Bank of America? "It's easy," says Marshall. "We can offer everything they can. What makes us more efficient is that we listen to our customers before we create and promote services that no one wants or needs. We keep our costs low, which allows us to invest more into our people and the community."

Part of the service the bank offers is informational, and part is just down-home personal. Most customers will have questions from time to time about how they can handle a particular money need. It may be a question about an investment, a payment schedule, or a credit life policy. Every owner—employee—is well-versed in handling these questions and helping the customer arrive at the best choice for their circumstances. If they are unsure of the best option, they bring in an owner with expertise in that area.

The personal touch is where service companies are differentiated. At Phelps County Bank, every owner strives to be a friend to every customer. They take time to look at the pictures of the new grand-baby, enjoy the latest hunting story, or just listen to the customer. They take time to build relationships, and they build trust.

Think about that for a minute. What is more important for an institution that holds all of your money than trust? Marshall says, "It doesn't matter how much we trust the customer, what is important is how much they trust us."

Marshall points out one other success strategy the bank uses. "We give back to our communities," he says. "We hope to hit $150,000 this year in direct community support. We sponsor the Take a Stand Against Child Abuse program, support the Center for Abused Women, help with Habitat for Humanity, and sponsor The Back Pack Project for poor children who can't afford school supplies and personal basics like toothbrushes and deodorant." The owners support dozens of other charitable causes too. "This is home, and we believe in giving back," Marshall says.

Changing a Changing Industry

In 1993, Gary Sage, founder of Sage Oil Vac, knew there had to be a better way to change oil. After one windy Texas Panhandle day, Sage returned to the house covered with oil and grime after servicing his seventeen irrigation engines.

Out of frustration, he designed, patented, and built a solution. His creation has become one of the hottest new items in the oil change industry.

Aaron Sage, chief operations officer and son of the founder, told us about the product and the company's success. "Our oil vacs eliminate spills during oil changes, keep contaminants out of the system, save the owners time and money, and are friendly to the environment," he says. "In the past four years we have experienced phenomenal growth as we've changed the industrial oil-change industry."

Aaron Sage told us about the essentials they have focused on to achieve their rapid but planned growth. "We know that our product line is the driving force behind our success, but even great products don't sell themselves. Dad [Gary Sage] handles the research and development, and we now have a fully integrated line of twenty-four different models," he says. "We also know that great companies surround themselves with outstanding people. From the manufacturing floor to the management team, we've hired the best."

Phillip Seidenberger, sales manager for Oil Vac, explained the power of becoming a master marketer. "We have no secret formulas," he says. "We use the basic marketing principles that all growing companies use to compete with bigger competitors. We build a quality line of products, save our customers time, money, and hassles, and back everything we sell with warranties and service."

The company has focused on building strategic relationships with large potential customers, diversifying into new and unrelated markets, and broadening their lines of product offerings. Seidenberger is quick to quantify the company's marketing success. "Our sales have increased by an annual percentage rate of more than 100 percent each year for the past three years," he says. "And we've only begun to tap the potential."

Aaron Sage details another success strategy that Oil Vac utilizes to achieve growth. "We know we need timely information to succeed. We produce monthly financial statements, and every quarter we meet with professional advisers," he says. "We review our progress, look for early trends, and anticipate problems."

Gary and Helen Sage have shared the good times and the bad times as the company has grown into a quality manufacturer. "We're still a small, family-owned business," Helen says. "It's hard to realize sometimes just how far we've come."

They have come a long way. From the cornfields of the Texas Panhandle, to serving customers like the U.S. Navy, ConocoPhillips, the U.S. Air Force, Bell Helicopter, and the Marine Corps, Sage Oil Vac has prospered despite fierce competition. Which once again reinforces that doing the right things, and doing them well, is a formula that will work for any type of business.

Sometimes It's All About Heart

Ken Dumminger, owner of Dumminger Photo in Fremont, Ohio, knows about heart. He knows about the hearts of friends and the hearts of people he hasn't even met. And he understands about the heart of a community.

However, for Dumminger the problem wasn't his heart, it was his liver. He was at the prime of his 33-year long career as a photographer and certified photographic consultant when a specialist determined that Dumminger's liver was in the final stages of failure. Without a transplant, he would die.

While he lay in the hospital waiting for a donor organ, it was business as usual at the store. The staff took heart and made the Christmas season a success. Family and friends helped out too. It was a good season despite the fact that Dumminger's life was ebbing away. "I didn't know what was going on," he says. "At that point I was just too sick to care."

Suddenly, on January 22, 2002, in a flurry of activity, a new liver arrived, and the long surgical process began. For Dumminger, it was the gift of life.

Gradually, he grew stronger and learned about the community support he had received as he lingered at death's door. The buckets of cards and letters, the hundreds of hours that volunteers had contributed, and the loyal customers who went right on shopping at Dumminger Photo just as they had before. He was amazed at the support of his community.

The 4-H kids traditionally worked the county fair as a fund-raiser for their club projects and events. Instead, they decided to help Dumminger catch up on medical bills and related expenses. They held a big bake sale, and passed through the grandstands collecting donations. When the dust settled they had raised more than $12,000.

"I couldn't fully understand the community's graciousness," Dumminger says. "All this for me? What did I ever do to earn that?"

However, to many community members and leaders, there was no mystery. You see, Dumminger has spent his life helping others. For thirty-three years prior to his illness, he helped people make memories. He taught youngsters how to load their first camera. He showed hobby photographers how to move up to professional grade. He helped everyone get more out of family keepsakes and irreplaceable photos. He was a giver, and when you give the gifts of love and service, they invariably come back.

Dumminger's key success strategies are: building lifetime relationships with customers, surrounding himself with quality people, getting it right the first time, and staying ahead of changes in the industry. "We don't sell photographic equipment and services, we make memories," Dumminger says. "Memories become more valuable as time passes. We like being a part of our customer's family history."

Dumminger put his heart into caring for his customers, and when the crisis came, his customers took care of him. "We're a stronger company than we were ten years ago," Dumminger says. "And it's because of loyal customers—they are the heart of our business."

Dumminger has a final message to share. "Become an organ donor," he encourages. "Every day people die because a suitable donor isn't found. You can give the gift of life."

Cleaning Up in the High-End Market

For Alex Giftos, business has always been a family affair. As a junior high student he began his career working at his father's vacuum repair shop. The company now owns two stores, one in Cadillac and one in Traverse City, Michigan.

"We're still a family operation," Giftos says of the stores. "My parents are still active in the businesses, and so is my wife."

However, unlike many small family-owned businesses, Cadillac Vacuum has pushed their operation to another level of success. "We try to stay on the cutting edge of our industry," says Giftos. "We are dedicated to our customer's long-term well-being."

For Cadillac Vacuum, steady growth in a challenging marketplace has come via four main areas of focus. Back in 1994, in the original *Up Against the Wal-Marts* book, we advocated "studying the success of others." Giftos has taken this success strategy to a new learning experience, via the Internet.

"I've benefited so much by attending the Vacuum Trade Dealers Association trade shows, and the informal dealer chats that occurred after the formal meetings were over every evening," he says. "I always have questions, and someone always has a good answer. That has really helped our business. The problem was that after the convention was over, I would often have questions that wouldn't wait until the next convention. I needed answers today." As a result of this need, Giftos and two friends, Cliff Brady and Justin Mellenbruch, launched an online association for vacuum dealers, suppliers, and manufacturers. "We share, we learn, we succeed," Giftos says. "The site was the missing link to learning from the success of others."

Giftos also believes in the power of finding a strong niche to work from. "We realized early on that the quick way out of business for independent vacuum dealers was to try to compete with Wal-Mart's and Kmart's low-end lines," he says. "Customers don't want cheap junk, they want value. We can show them how to get carpets cleaner, protect the investment they've made in their home, and lower the annual cost of owning a vacuum." Cadillac Vacuum carries top-of-the-line equipment, supports it with parts and service, and then educates the customers on the value and benefits of owning the best.

Giftos writes a regular column titled "The Way I See It" for the *Floor Care Professional Magazine*. Therein he passes along marketing, sales, and promotion tips for readers. "It's important to help the customer when they come in your front door, but it's more critical to get them there in the first place," he says. "We attract customers with our excellent repair and service and abundant inventory." The company carries nearly a hundred units in stock.

A final thing that Cadillac vacuum focuses on is being results-oriented. "We love to sell," he says. "But you've also got to count the beans and get the job done."

When Giftos finds the stress of retail closing in on him, he heads for the woods. His home is located on eighty acres of Michigan's wilderness, and he finds it's easy to forget his problems there. "It's our sanctuary," Giftos says. "We try to leave our problems at the stores and bring our family relationships home. It seems to be working."

Key Points Checklist

- ☑ The business owners we've profiled in this chapter are ordinary men and women just like you.

- ☑ They have achieved extraordinary results despite hypercompetition by doing the right things and doing them well.

- ☑ The right things are the success strategies from Chapter Two. They are utilizing these strategies to achieve double- and even triple-digit growth, build wealth, and improve all aspects of their operations.

☑ They also give back to their communities. They serve and support community programs and organizations.

☑ Though they represent some of the most successful businesses in their respective industries, these owners are still focused on improving their businesses and serving their customers more effectively.

The Kaizen Strategy

CHAPTER 11

The largest room in the world is the room for improvement.
—UNKNOWN

The Japanese word *Kaizen* (Ky'zen) means *continuous improvement involving everyone*. Its premise is straightforward: Everything can be improved, and it's everyone's job to do it.

In the late Sam Walton's autobiography, *Made in America*, David Glass, Wal-Mart's CEO, talked about his friend and boss. Glass said that Walton "gets up every day bound and determined to improve something." If improvement was important to the founder of the world's largest retailer, it should be important to us.

Kaizen *must* spread throughout every small business. Why? Because the big-box merchants, megachains, category killers, and lean independents have issued a challenge: *Get better or perish*. Your survival and future success will depend on your ability to make improvements in every aspect of your business.

Look for Kaizen ideas when you visit competitors' stores. You must learn from others, because as Oliver Goldsmith said, "People seldom improve when they have no model but themselves to copy after."

You will find in this chapter some overlap with material discussed in detail in other chapters. We do not apologize for the duplication. Some messages are important enough to be repeated. We want you to use this chapter as a tool for developing your own Kaizen strategy.

We hope you will implement many of the tactics we give you, but you'll need to go beyond our thoughts and add your own. Your associates may have some great ideas on how you can improve in several areas. Get them involved.

Start today. Don't just read this chapter and go on as usual. Instead, when you read a Kaizen tactic that would improve something in your business, put it to work *now*. There is a Chinese proverb that says, "A journey of a thousand miles begins with a single step." Take that step now.

Kaizen Tactics: 292 Powerful Suggestions for Improving Your Business

For your convenience, we have listed these improvement tactics in specific categories. You may wish to start by reviewing the Kaizen tactics in your weakest areas.

Kaizen and Your Customers

1. Talk to customers every day. Spend time on the sales floor. Ask your customers how you're doing in terms of meeting their needs.

2. Talk to your twenty-five largest customers every month.

3. Contact former customers as soon as you learn they are *former* customers. Find out why they stopped doing business with you. Correct the problems when you find out what they are.

4. Develop your own customer profile.

5. Count potential customers every day. If people are walking into your business in increasing numbers, your promotion strategies are probably working.

6. Compute your Customer Batting Average (total walk-in traffic divided by the number who make purchases).

7. Set goals to improve your customer batting average.

8. Compute the dollar volume of your average sale (total sales divided by the number of purchases).

9. Train your staff in the art of *suggestive,* or *add-on, selling* and set goals to increase the average sale.

10. Learn your customers' names. Remember, all business is *personal.* Learn just one customer's name each day, and you'll gain more than 300 new names every year!

11. Call your customers by their names.

12. Greet customers as soon as they enter your business. Make eye contact and smile.

13. Inspire your employees to provide great customer service by being their example. Your customer *attitude* is a powerful motivator for your team.

14. Build your business with courteous, professional telephone techniques. Don't spend $1,000 on Yellow Page ads and then blow it when the phone rings.

15. Conduct a customer survey to find areas to improve.

16. Find out when your competitors are open for business.

17. Find out when your customers want to shop. (Ask them.)

18. Change your open-for-business hours to provide plenty of hours for your customers' convenient shopping.

19. Keep your promises. If you say you'll open at 9:00 a.m., open at 9:00 a.m., not at 9:03, 9:06, or 9:17.

20. Make certain every employee attends at least one customer-service training program every year.

21. Calculate the dollar value of every potential customer and post it for all employees to see. Keep them focused on the importance of the customer.

22. Thank all customers for their business. You need them; they don't need you.

23. If you sell big-ticket items—$100 or more—follow up after every sale. Following up shows that you care, that you want them to be fully satisfied, and that you appreciate their business.

24. If you sell small-ticket items, follow up with repeat customers. Let them know you value their business.

25. Take every opportunity to subtly point out to your customers the benefits of doing business with you.

26. Solicit customer suggestions.

27. Give customers public recognition for useful ideas. A plaque, special mention in your newsletter, or a picture in your print ads is a nice way to say thanks.

28. Set aside a bonus kitty for employees who are taking good care of customers. For example, set aside $100 per month for $10 above-and-beyond awards.

29. Give verbal praise and financial reward to any employee who generates such outstanding service that your customers inform you about it.

30. Considering new products? Ask your ten best customers what they think about them. They will be flattered and may tell others that you have the items (if you decide to carry them).

31. When you have a walk-in customer who *just wants to look around*, ask for their opinion on a new product. You may not make a direct sale, but the customer will feel involved and will see some of what you have to sell.

32. If any of your customers are businesses, offer them free *advertising* space in your newsletter. It's a great way to thank folks who do business with you.

33. Put your home phone number on your business card. Some customers may be impressed because you're accessible.

Kaizen Your Costs (Eliminate Waste)

34. Take time to do every job right the first time. (If there isn't time to do it right, where will you find the time to do it over?)

35. Remember that everything is negotiable.

36. Reduce overhead costs as a percentage of sales.

37. When you look at expenses to reduce, analyze your largest expense categories first. A small reduction percentage-wise in a large category may be worth more than a 20 or 30 percent reduction in a small one.

38. Strive to reduce your costs of goods sold. Better buying means easier selling.

39. Check every expense category on your income statement against businesses of similar size in your industry.

40. Set goals to bring your expenses to a position of "better than your industry average."

41. Don't ignore small expense categories. A dollar saved is a dollar earned. Costs that you eliminate drop dollar for dollar to your bottom line.

42. Install energy-saving lightbulbs and fixtures.

43. Put timers on your thermostats.

44. Change furnace and air conditioner filters regularly.

45. Insulate for heating and cooling savings. Energy savings can pay for itself in months.

46. Put timers on your lights.

47. Ask your utility suppliers for other money-saving tips.

48. Don't buy long-distance service from the first company to make a pitch for your business. Get all the details.

49. Eliminate fancy add-on telephone services.

50. Use the phone book instead of directory assistance at 50 cents per call. Let your fingers walk for themselves. Don't use the automatic dialing service provided by directory assistance. It's too expensive.

51. If you're traveling, don't have calls billed to your room. You'll often pay more than double the going rate.

52. Check your phone service provider to see if a call waiting option is less expensive than adding a new line. (You may also be able to eliminate an existing line.)

53. Plan your calls. Use a checklist to cover the major points, then get off the phone. You can lower your phone bill and save time.

54. Lower your postage costs by e-mailing whenever you can.

55. Eliminate overnight deliveries whenever possible. Use e-mail or fax, and mail the follow-up.

56. Use two-day delivery services and save big over the cost of overnight. (Plan ahead and save a lot.)

57. Combine mailings. If you send several pieces to the same company every day, put them together when you can.

58. Buy lighter-weight mailers, envelopes, and paper. Eliminate a second stamp and save nearly 60 percent.

59. Clean up your direct mail lists. It's not uncommon to have 10 percent duplication and error rates.

60. Cull the list for every mailing. Not all customers on your list may be targets for a particular offer.

61. Check to see if there's a "pre-sort" company in your area who combines mailings from small businesses.

62. Eliminate the fax cover sheet. Instead, use the small transmittal notices in the margins of your first page.

63. Transmit bulk faxes and other telephone data when the rates are lowest—usually after 11:00 p.m.

64. Check the costs of printing versus copying. In quantity, printing may be less expensive.

65. Make two-sided copies. You can save postage and paper.

66. When printing, check prices every time.

67. Watch the cost of service contracts. Renew for one year at a time or eliminate most of them. A copier may be an exception if a service contract is cost-effective.

68. Store office supplies together. Avoid duplication by keeping a list in the storage area of what's on hand.

69. Buy seasonal supplies in the off-season.

70. Print high-quality color letterhead to use for customers, prospects, and clients. Use an inexpensive black-and-white version for other purposes.

71. Reward employees who make money-saving suggestions. Encourage thrifty ideas.

72. Use a graphic artist instead of an ad agency to help you design a logo, letterhead, or brochures.

73. When taking your artist-designed work to a printer, try to negotiate for the 10 to 15 percent rebate commission an ad agency would get from the printer as well.

74. Save your time and money by letting a travel agent find the best rates for travel.

75. Clean your own windows (often).

76. Do your own janitorial work (or offer to let your employees earn a little extra).

77. Try to find a retired maintenance person to handle minor electrical, plumbing, and carpentry repairs. It's a win-win situation.

78. Don't buy "new" when "used" will do. This applies to property, fixtures, equipment, and furniture.

79. Buy used vehicles. Be patient. Let several dealers know what you're looking for and wait. Check national repair records before selecting a model or brand.

80. Maintain your vehicles regularly and extend their useful life. Keep them clean and instruct your drivers to drive courteously. Your image is at stake.

81. Use colorful signs on your vehicles and get more mileage out of your advertising.

82. Lower the cost of outside accounting and legal services by doing more of your work in-house.

83. Write your own contracts and have your attorney look them over.

84. Organize your own accounting information in an orderly manner and save on the professional's time.

85. Review all professional and insurance costs annually. Make certain all charges are correct and fair.

86. Cut insurance costs by eliminating unneeded coverage.

87. Raise insurance deductibles to lower rates. You should never insure for losses you can afford to take.

88. Have your insurance coverage bid every two or three years. Companies and rates change. Don't get into the rut of automatic renewal.

89. Manage your workers' compensation costs with careful monitoring and safety programs. Make sure all job classifications are accurate. Incorrect risk assessments can double or triple rates.

90. Save money by refinancing debt. Refinancing can lower payments, free up cash, or shorten repayment times.

91. Work with your banker to consolidate installment notes, credit cards, and credit lines to lower rate packages.

92. Monitor service charges and fees from your financial institution. Ask why you're being charged. It may be a mistake. Shop around; if others offer free services, negotiate. Move accounts as a last resort.

93. Don't let checking account balances sit idle. Get an interest-bearing account.

94. Negotiate credit card processing fees. If the volume has increased, you may be able to get a lower rate. Consider electronic processing options.

95. Monitor credit card usage in your business. You may be able to eliminate low-usage, high-cost cards.

96. Cut payroll costs by reducing pay-period frequency. Going to biweekly or monthly payroll periods can free up administrative hours for more important work.

97. Consult with a tax professional to reduce taxes or keep your tax payments working longer for you. The rules are complex, but an expert can often save you money.

98. Use outside contractors instead of employees when the costs are lower. Consider the cost of benefits, FICA, withholding, and so on.

99. Let your employees pick up some of the increasing health care costs. This has a twofold benefit: (1) It gives the employees—who otherwise often take it for granted—a better sense of the value of the benefit, and (2) It allows you to cap your costs.

100. Consider adding part-time help instead of paying overtime.

101. Cut the costs of benefits with flexible spending accounts for your employees. Check with a tax pro for details.

102. Check with your trade association, Chamber of Commerce, or other businesses organization to see if group insurance policies are available to lower costs.

103. Consider employee-leasing options.

104. Take every trade discount you're entitled to.

105. Make fewer purchases of larger volume to capture volume discounts or free freight offers.

106. Consider joining a barter exchange. Try to trade your products or services for others you buy regularly. You save the difference between cost and retail.

107. Trade cost-saving ideas with other businesses like yours. We know a business owner who jotted down her ten best cost-saving ideas and sent the list to ten other small business owners. Within a month, she had received more than thirty additional ideas in return.

108. Don't forget to add all capital purchases to your fixed asset list so you can take the depreciation deduction.

109. Read the expense deduction part of the IRS's Small Businesses Tax Guide (publication 334). Don't miss deducting any expenses.

110. Use your employees in slow seasons to do work you would otherwise have to pay others for. We know an appliance dealer who used his employees to completely remodel the interior of his store. It was a pleasant break from the routine, ensured job security, and saved the owner thousands of dollars.

111. Consider luxury expenses like leased luxury cars, Rolex watches, and first-class travel carefully. These may be good for your ego, but it's bad business practice.

112. Recycle for savings. Use the back of unused copies for printing rough drafts.

113. Reuse laser printer cartridges and save as much as 50 percent of the cost of new.

114. Reink printer ribbons.

115. Reuse floppy disks.

116. Reverse file folders and use them again.

117. Use refillable pens and pencils.

118. Recycle aluminum cans, cardboard, and paper. Donate to non-profit organizations for publicity if there are no direct cost benefits.

119. Reuse mailers and shipping containers when your image isn't at stake.

120. Invest in a sign-making machine or graphics software to reduce outside printing and design costs.

121. Cut out nonperforming advertising. Better yet, invest this money in promotions that work.

122. Measure the performance of your advertising. Use different offers for print as opposed to electronic ads. When customers ask for the special offer, you'll know the source. (This allows you to measure the effectiveness of different advertising mediums.)

123. Every lease should be renegotiated when it comes due. Shop around; use comparable space (dollars per square foot, and so on) to improve your negotiating position.

124. Using an advertising agency? Push for a lower commission.

125. Using janitorial or lawn-care services? Trim the costs or find alternatives. One owner cut 50 percent off lawn-care services by hiring an employee's son.

126. Right-size your labor force. Inefficient or unproductive employees can drain your profits.

127. Trim promotion costs by training everyone to promote your business. When you deliver your products or services, have delivery personnel pass out business cards and flyers to neighboring businesses.

128. Avoid the cost of collection companies by making your own collection calls to delinquent accounts. (Calls are many more times effective than letters.) After you call, follow up in writing as a reminder.

Kaizen Your Associates

129. Empower your employees with Kaizen understanding. Discuss this chapter with them. Show them the importance of continuing improvement.

130. Create a Kaizen incentive or reward program. Pay for every valid improvement strategy your employees submit to you in writing. Offer plaques, money, time off, or other appropriate rewards.

131. Discuss the financial condition of your business with your employees. Help them understand their stake in its success. When they feel like they are a part of your business, their contributions will increase.

132. Create written job descriptions for every type of employee you need. List special personality traits and skills required for each job.

133. Next, review your present employees. Are current staff members well-matched for the jobs they have? Can you improve some of the matches? If some employees aren't good matches for anything, they might be happier working for another company.

134. Evaluate everyone in your company every year. Let them know how they are doing on a formal basis. Don't forget to praise good behavior whenever you see it.

135. Recognize good work from your associates. Look for unique ways to reward those who excel.

136. Always recognize an associate's personal best. Any new "high" deserves public acknowledgment.

137. Don't neglect your most talented workers to devote more time to less talented staff members. *All* employees need your time, encouragement, and leadership.

138. Let your more talented workers mentor (tutor) employees who need improvement.

139. Surround yourself with people more talented than yourself. Steel magnate Andrew Carnegie has this epitaph on his tombstone: "Here lies a man who knew how to enlist in his service better men than himself."

140. Delegate new tasks every month. Your employees will appreciate the added confidence and responsibility, and you will have more time to devote to other tasks.

141. Make a checklist (who, what, when, where, and so on) so you can monitor delegated tasks.

142. Take time every day to *listen* to your staff.

143. Take time every day to *talk* to your staff.

144. Involve key employees in major decisions.

145. Give all employees their own business cards.

146. Praise publicly.

147. Criticize privately.

148. Remember that employees won't earn you very much until they are well-trained.

149. Cross-train key employees.

150. Remember, people satisfy customers.

151. Employees make first impressions for your business. Encourage them to dress conservatively so they will not offend any customer. Invest in uniforms, vests, or smocks to create a more professional appearance.

152. Set a good example by dressing professionally yourself.

153. Be specific in explaining how you expect your employees to dress for work.

154. Compliment associates who dress appropriately.

155. Provide opportunities for personal growth.

156. Pay for training when employees complete a course.

157. Encourage skill building, whether or not it's job-related.

158. Teach by example the career benefits of telling the truth, keeping your word, taking responsibility for your actions, planning and prioritizing every day, and keeping the workplace organized.

159. Focus on finding solutions, not detailing problems.

Kaizen Your Salesmanship

160. Don't say no for your customer. Present the best value you can offer, and let them decide.

161. Read *Selling the Invisible* by Harry Beckwith. You'll get a new perspective on selling services that will help you sell anything.

162. When the products and services you sell are similar to those of your competitors, sell the *differences*.

163. Customers are experts at knowing when they feel valued and appreciated. Salespeople who enjoy helping others, take time to build relationships, and really get to know their customers will achieve selling success.

164. People will tell you what they think about your offer . . . if you ask.

165. Before your sales staff can sell anything to anyone, they have to be sold on it themselves.

166. Don't overpromise to get the sale. You may lose the customer. Instead, sell the facts. The mark of a professional is measured in reorders.

167. Remember that even the best products must be sold. Seldom will you have anyone just come in and take it away from you.

168. An average salesperson tells. A good salesperson explains. A great salesperson inspires buyers to see the benefits as their own.

169. In service selling, you're not making a sale, you're creating a customer.

170. Knowing that your sales are increasing isn't as important as knowing why.

171. Don't lose the sale by overusing your mouth. In Texas we say, "Don't let your tongue slit your throat."

172. Understand that sales competition comes from anyone going after the same dollar you are. For example, grocery stores don't just compete with other grocery stores. They compete for the food dollar. Who's competing for the same dollar as you?

173. People do business with people they are comfortable with. In sales, it pays to make people like you.

174. There are few places where courtesy reaps greater rewards than in selling.

175. Learn the art of service selling, and money will follow you wherever you go.

176. We all live by selling something. An author sells knowledge, inspiration, or entertainment. A doctor sells health and well-being. A cosmetic manufacturer sells hope. Car companies sell dependable transportation and status. What are you selling?

177. Your goal as a salesperson is to sell goods that don't come back, to people who will.

178. A fool can sell if the price is low enough.

179. Ask for the business.

Kaizen Your Banking Relationship

180. Get copies of your personal and business credit reports annually. Correct them *before* you visit your banker.

181. Let your banker know how you're doing, even when you don't need to borrow money.

182. Take copies of your financial statements to your banker at least once per year. If you've had a great quarter—share those statements too.

183. Arrange for working capital—a line of credit—before you need it. You can negotiate better terms when you're not in dire need.

184. Get approval for more than you need.

185. Never borrow more on your line of credit than you need.

186. When you need to arrange long-term borrowing, be prepared. Anticipate the banker's three basic questions: (1) How much do you need? (2) What do you need it for? (3) How will you pay it back?

187. Take projected financial statements to show your repayment ability based on anticipated profits. Don't forget to include a cash flow statement. Bankers love cash flow; you should too.

188. Be prepared to answer questions about your projections.

189. Remember that banks are like rental car companies. Car companies rent you a car, charge for every day you use it, and expect to get the car back. Banks rent money, charge interest, and expect repayment of principal.

190. Remember, all bank terms are negotiable.

191. Educate your banker. Share relevant trade articles on your industry. Give them a copy of any good publicity your business receives.

192. Get to know several people at your bank, people with varying levels of responsibility. Then, if your main contact leaves, you won't be a complete unknown.

193. Introduce your key employees to your banker.

194. Invite your banker to visit your business.

195. Invite your banker to do business with you.

196. Introduce potential customers to your banker.

197. Recommend your bank to employees and associates.

198. Evaluate your business using the six "C's" of credit:

    ▪ *Character*—Your personal integrity and repayment history. Perhaps the most important determinant.

    ▪ *Capacity*—Your company's financial strength and repayment ability.

    ▪ *Confidence*—Your attitude and belief in your own ability. You should appear self-assured.

    ▪ *Capital*—Your debt-to-equity ratio. Your ability to secure other equity sources.

    ▪ *Conditions*—The area economy and the condition of your industry.

    ▪ *Collateral*—Assets that you own and your backup repayment sources.

199. Remember, in borrowing, risk is responsible for rate. The better risk you are, the better rate you get.

Kaizen Your Technology

200. Add a Web site to your marketing strategy.

201. Remember, the goals of a good Web site are: attracting customers, enhancing your image, and providing useful information.

202. Use your e-mail, Web, and surface mail addresses, phone and fax numbers, and logo on all marketing materials.

203. Use your Web site to answer frequently asked questions (FAQs).

204. If you use e-mail to reach customers and potential customers, get their permission first. Don't spam.

205. Send out an electronic newsletter. Give your customers "news they can use."

206. Make your Web site interactive. Encourage feedback.

207. If you do special events at your business, post them on a "what's happening" calendar on your Web site.

208. Keep your Web site fresh with frequent updates.

209. Consider adding a "tip of the day" to your Web site.

210. When you compete with a Web site, you can be as colorful, professional, and effective as any big-box competitor.

211. Don't let slow-loading graphics drive customers away. Web experts recommend that your home page should load in under eight seconds. Time goes fast in cyberspace.

212. Reassure your online customers about site security.

213. Use your Web presence to reinforce the benefits you offer your customers.

214. Use a consistent design on all of your marketing materials, including your Web site.

215. Remember, a good Web page is like a good print ad. You should keep it simple, with lots of white space.

216. Use your computer to track financial performance, customer data, and other business information.

217. Check your trade publications for hardware and software recommendations for your type of business.

218. Be certain that what you buy is upgradeable and compatible.

219. Invest in point-of-purchase scanners if you haven't already. Bar code reading systems are very affordable.

220. Look into marketing databases that might help you identify potential customers.

221. Use your computer to help you monitor and manage inventory.

222. Generate customized and personalized mailing lists for current and potential customers.

223. Learn to use the "mail-merge" function of your word processing software to save time on large mailings.

224. Use custom label-making packages to save time and give professional-looking results.

225. Consider getting "on-line" with your suppliers.

226. Use invoicing and billing software packages to speed up accounts receivable collection.

227. Use sign-making software to create great-looking signs.

228. Use a professional graphics artist to help you create classy brochures, newsletters, and marketing materials.

229. Get a toll-free phone number.

230. Check out customer-management software.

Kaizen Your Pricing

231. Remember, to sell it right, you've got to buy it right.

232. Check out the buying groups that serve your industry. Get the details and then talk to members. Some save as much as 8 percent on cost of goods sold.

233. Make a list of ten items that your competitors are selling better than you can. Call your suppliers to see what they can do.

234. Locate at least three new buying sources this year.

235. Put a variable pricing system into practice today.

236. Get close to your competitors on price-sensitive items.

237. Make up profit margin on your blind items.

238. Put prices on inventory in your store. Customers complain that the new breed doesn't do this.

239. When you make a great buy on merchandise, pass some of the savings on to your customers. This practice will help you improve your "value perception."

Kaizen Your Financial Statements

240. If you aren't already, begin producing and analyzing financial statements every month.

241. Get composite financial statements from your trade association so you can have a benchmark for yours.

242. Set goals to increase your sales by a specific amount this year.

243. Communicate those goals with everyone in your business.

244. Record your progress toward your goals every day, every week, and every month. Make it a game. Keep score.

245. Establish goals to improve your profit by a specific amount. (Read "Kaizen Your Costs" and "Kaizen Your Pricing," both above.)

246. Reduce your accounts receivable as a percentage of your sales.

247. Reduce your accounts receivable collection time.

248. Take all discounts offered on invoices.

249. Analyze profit margins on the different lines you sell.

250. Promote the lines with the highest margins to increase your overall margin.

251. Try to decrease your inventory as a percentage of sales every year.

252. Try to turn your inventory more times than your industry's average.

253. Reduce your debt-to-equity ratio.

254. Common-size your financial statements for the last three years. Look for trends. (See Chapter Nine.)

255. Work hard to improve your current ratio (liquidity).

256. Produce a cash flow statement, and monitor where your cash is going.

257. Lower your cost of goods sold percentage by buying better and pricing right.

258. Know your cash position, and try to lower your expenses to improve your position.

Kaizen Resources

259. Get ideas for improving your business from other businesses like yours in other trade areas. Visit their stores; invite them to yours.

260. Visit your library at least once each month. Go during a slow morning or afternoon, and look for new books on topics related to your business.

261. While at the library, pick out two or three trade publications in industries unrelated to your own. Look for improvement ideas to borrow.

262. Read advertisements in out-of-town newspapers.

263. When you network with other businesspeople, go armed with some questions, such as, What's the most successful promotion you ever had? or, If you were in my shoes, how would you try to get more customers?

264. Attend trade shows and industry meetings. If you can't attend, get tapes of relevant seminars and speeches.

265. Visit your state fair and spend a day talking to business vendors and exhibitors. Observe the displays.

266. Visit the megastores regularly. They are the cutting edge—see what's new.

267. Contact your trade association for training materials, publications, and recent studies.

268. Visit your local bookstore. Try to find at least one book with new ideas.

269. Visit with college or university business deans, department heads, and professors.

Personal Kaizen

270. Read *Over the Top* by Zig Ziglar.

271. Build your personal communication skills by joining a Toastmaster's club. (Learn to speak, listen, and think on your feet.)

272. Get computer-smart. Training is cheap, and the rewards are great.

273. Listen to motivational tapes while you are traveling.

274. Read *How to Win Friends and Influence People* by Dale Carnegie. It's sixty-seven years old and still right on target.

275. Write down three personal desires you want to accomplish this year. Answer questions like, "I've always wanted to . . . ," or "I'd like to learn . . . ."

276. Spend some time with someone who understands and uses the goal-setting process in his/her life.

277. Set at least one personal goal to achieve this year in the following areas: spiritual renewal, physical renewal, family relationships, career growth, education, and finances.

278. Read *Seeds of Greatness* by Denis Waitley.

279. Resolve to improve your physical fitness. A little conditioning can improve your health, restore vitality, increase mental alertness, and improve your attitude.

280. Read the Bible. You'll find business wisdom and knowledge, particularly in the Book of Proverbs, regardless of your faith.

281. Take a course in the art of negotiating. Learn how to create win-win situations.

282. Spend one hour alone every week doing something you really enjoy.

283. Divide a clean white sheet of paper into two columns. List your strengths on the left and your weaknesses on the right. Pick two weaknesses to turn into strengths this year.

284. Nurture your family and friendships.

285. Don't fear failure. Most successful people experience failure before success.

286. Surround yourself with funny people. Laughter is good for your soul and is a terrific stress reliever.

287. Take your work seriously, but don't take yourself too seriously. The world will go on after we're gone. Try to enjoy the time you have. Happiness is not in the destination, but in the journey itself.

288. Accentuate the possible. Since we become what we think about, emphasize the possible.

289. Never say any of the following: "I can't," "I quit," "I'll get even," or "That won't work; I tried it once."

290. Say these words often: "I can," "I will," "I love you," "I'll help," and "What can I do?"

291. Live every day as if there were no tomorrow. We have no guarantee, except that we shall reap whatever we sow. Today's decisions are tomorrow's realities.

292. Mistakes are the building blocks of experience. Experience is the foundation of success. Don't be afraid of making mistakes, but don't stop there. Use each mistake as a step toward success.

Key Points Checklist

- ☑ Everything can be improved.
- ☑ It is everyone's job to see that improvements are made.
- ☑ Select at least ten areas where you will make improvements this year.
- ☑ Look for improvement ideas everywhere you go.

Beating Burnout CHAPTER 12

When it is dark enough, you can see the stars.
—RALPH WALDO EMERSON

Tears rolled down his face as he watered the bare-root nursery stock in the bins. The rock wall behind the bins was a 100-year-old work of art. But this day the wall and the trees themselves were a blur behind the tears of frustration.

He had closed the store an hour earlier, at 7 P.M. It had been a long, bitter day. The fight he had had with his wife had been the culmination of what he'd been feeling for weeks.

The man's name was Don, and he had just celebrated his thirty-fourth birthday. He and his wife had opened the lawn and garden store nearly four years earlier. It was the realization of his dream to own his own business.

The work had been hard, the hours long, and it had taken two years to make a profit. Except for the money Don and his wife had used to purchase their home, every dime they owned was tied up in the business.

But this day Don would have walked away from it all. All the hours and all the effort seemed a waste. His dream now seemed more like a nightmare. It was a nightmare with no end, no way out. He had built the trap, and now he was caught in it.

He could still see the hurt in his wife's eyes as he had lashed out at her. She had been blindsided by his anger. She probably wondered what she had done to cause the outburst.

Sue was the light of his life. He hadn't meant to take it out on her. After all, she had worked just as hard as he had to make the store a success. He loved her with all his heart, how could he have been so unkind to her?

Don wiped his eyes, and moved to another bin. He still had another hour's work to do. Suddenly he felt exhausted. He wanted to go home and play with his three-year-old daughter. He wanted to tell Sue how sorry he was and hold her in his arms. But instead, he dragged out the watering hose and began wetting down the bedding plants. The plants couldn't wait. They needed water. Customers who came at 7 A.M. the next day wouldn't buy plants that were wilted.

As he moved to the flats of tomatoes, Don wondered how his dream had come to this. He and Sue hadn't had a vacation since he had left his corporate job. Weekends blurred into weekdays, and except for Sunday morning church services, almost every waking hour was spent at the store.

Saturdays were the busiest days. Though the store was closed on Sunday, it was rare that Don wasn't there catching up on the dozens of things that he hadn't gotten done during the week. He had even worked on Thanksgiving Day, putting the finishing touches on the Christmas decorations at the store.

As he watered the flats of petunias, Don didn't see the beauty of the pink and purple blooms. He was thinking about the past Christmas Eve. He had kept the store open until 8 P.M. as a service for last-minute shoppers.

Christi, his three-year-old, had already gone to bed before he had gotten home. He had been exhausted, but still had a dollhouse to put together before he could rest. He had fallen asleep with the screwdriver in his hand and the dollhouse half-finished.

Spring had been late in coming, and when it came, the rush hit all at once. It had been a record spring saleswise, but as a result, the "to do" list Don kept on his desk had turned into pages. He was putting out the fires and taking care of customers, but it wasn't fun anymore.

Don turned off the water and coiled the hose at the base of the hydrant. He sat down on a pile of landscape timbers and felt alone. He wondered if other business owners in town ever felt this way.

Tomorrow was Saturday. The weather was ideal for spring plant-ing, and there would be customers standing outside when he arrived at a quarter to seven. Don dreaded the coming day.

A True Story

The story we used to open this chapter is true. The Don we wrote about is our coauthor Don Taylor. The burnout was real. It happened nearly twenty-five years ago, but Don remembers the day we de-scribed as if it were last week.

"That was the lowest point of my business career," Don said. "I had worked harder at making that first store a success than anything I'd ever done. That day, it seemed like the business had become a millstone around my neck. I would have walked away if Sue and I hadn't had everything we owned invested in that business."

Don's story has a happy ending. He worked his way through the period of burnout and eventually sold the business to another young entrepreneur. The lessons learned from that experience were burned indelibly into his brain. They became the basis for helping hundreds of business owners just like you, who may be experiencing a personal slump.

The Bad News

Burnout happens to everyone. We experience periods in our life when things pile up and we slow down. We seem to be working harder than ever before, but getting less done.

Little irritations that we once blew off now hound us. The piles are growing, and we spend more time sifting through the mounds than doing actual work. We find it hard to focus on the most important tasks. The quality of management we once prided ourselves on is now missing. Customers are becoming an annoyance. Our employees are growing less competent every day. The business we once loved has become a burden.

We seem to slip into a mental fog. We want to quit. Unfortunately, we have too much invested—in both money and pride—to just walk away. So we grind ahead, sometimes halfheartedly, but plodding onward.

The magic is gone. The fun we once had running this business has turned into drudgery. We feel alone and are hesitant to talk to anyone about it. We wonder if we're depressed. We can't understand how this can be normal. We're usually more positive and upbeat.

The Good News

The good news is that you are normal and certainly not alone. All of us, even the most successful business owners, have periods of time when it seems that we are walking under our own personal cloud.

The good news is that these tough times never last, but tough people do. Remember the wise words, "This too shall pass."

Life always runs in cycles. For every down cycle, there is an up cycle. The hardest part is hanging on when the cycle hits bottom. And yet that is exactly what we have to do.

Sometimes we only have to look around us to see people worse off than we are to begin to realize we don't have it so bad. Counting your blessings can often provide a beginning to your recovery from a period of burnout.

But if you can't see anyone else's problems because your own seem so big, do not despair. Most business owners who experience burnout do not end up in padded cells. Instead, they learn to manage the causes of burnout and often end up with a stronger business and a better understanding of how to avoid recurrences.

To speed you along the road to recovering your zest for your work, we have assembled a fifteen-step plan. These steps will help you dig your way out of the burnout bog and get your motivational juices flowing once more.

The Fifteen-Step Plan for Beating Burnout

Step One—*Be patient and take time to have some fun.* You didn't get to this stage of burnout in a day or a week. It will take some time to turn things around to a point where you begin to see progress and feel real excitement again.

The key to a faster recovery is to start rekindling the fire right now. Once you know the feelings you have been experiencing are those of classic burnout, you can deal with them.

Benjamin Franklin said, "He that can have patience can have what he will." Don't be disappointed if you don't feel better tomorrow. Just relax and be assured that as you follow these steps, burnout will become less and less of a problem.

Bill Marshall of Phelps County Bank in Rolla, Missouri, understands the role of humor in diffusing stress and burnout. "We make fun a part of our workday," he says. "We have fun with our customers and fun among ourselves. A great way to beat burnout is to have as much fun as you can."

Step Two—*Be Positive.* Your success in business is 10 percent what happens to you and 90 percent what you choose to do about it. No one has ever beaten a bad case of burnout with a negative attitude. Be positive.

Taking a positive attitude to work every day is a matter of choice. It is your choice. No one can make you have a bad day unless you allow him or her to. You are in charge of your own attitude. Jerrold Taylor, of Monet De Sauw, says, "There are only two choices in how we approach life: We can choose to be positive, or we can allow others to make us negative. Being positive pays better."

W. Clement Stone said, "There is little difference in people . . . the little difference is attitude. The big difference is whether it is positive or negative." Be positive.

Step Three—*Avoid Negative People.* I don't believe that anyone experiencing burnout should isolate themselves from their friends and loved ones. But you must insulate yourself from negative people.

Maintaining a positive attitude is a fragile proposition when you're in a personal slump. So don't allow yourself to be bombarded by pessimists. Every unhappy person in the world would like to drag you down to his or her level of unhappiness. Remember, misery loves company.

When George Wilder of the Locker Room finds himself headed for a slump, he seeks out a specific group of people: "I get around folks that I can learn from and that are high-energy individuals. Soon I find myself reenergized and ready to tackle the world."

Step Four—*Eliminate Physical Causes.* One of the first things to do when you hit a slump is to determine if there's a physical reason. Are you eating right? Do you get regular exercise? Are you getting enough rest? How long has it been since your last thorough physical checkup?

When it comes to your health, little things can add up. We all need healthier foods. If you take the skin off fried chicken, you cut the fat in half. Eat a small second helping of vegetables instead of dessert. When you feel stress at work, take a short walk. Even fifteen minutes can help you get the blood circulating to your brain again.

Reduce or eliminate the consumption of alcohol and tobacco products. Get a good checkup and follow your doctor's advice. If you spend most of your day in passive activities, you'll sleep better with some exercise. Yes, every little thing matters when you're battling burnout.

Step Five—*Review Your Goals.* When you feel rotten and you've lost your focus, it's time to review your goals. Every one of us needs to be reminded of what is really important in our lives. From time to time we need to review our objectives. When all that you can see is the problem at hand, it may be time to sit down with your goals and remind yourself why they are important to you. It works.

Bill Boyd, a partner in Java Coffee and Tea Company in Houston, told us how he overcomes burnout. "I just think back to what I used to do for a living," he said. "I don't want to go back, and that makes me feel better about what I'm doing now."

You can beat the blues by refocusing on what you really want. When you remind yourself of those things that are really important to you, you'll often find a little extra resolve.

Step Six—*Destroy the Piles.* If you're an average business owner, you have piles. If you've been battling burnout for some time, you have even more piles. To get back in the groove, clear the clutter.

Here's a system that works. *First,* clear your desk or work area even if you set stuff on the floor. Now divide the clutter into three piles: *Pile A*—Items that require your personal attention, are of critical importance, and have short deadlines; *Pile B*—Items that need your attention, but not right now; and *Pile C*—Items that need your attention, but can wait. Throw everything else away. When in doubt, throw it out.

Now go back to *Pile A.* Cull this pile to four or five highest priorities. Place the rest of *Pile A* on top of *Pile B.* Put all of your attention and energy into the highest priorities. When you've cleared them, pick the next four or five priorities and repeat the process. It may take a few days, but it works. When you destroy the piles, you'll feel better about the progress you're making.

Step Seven—*Eliminate Distractions.* The only thing that "multi-taskers" are really good at is lying about how good they are at multi-tasking. Pulling yourself out of the burnout bog will require focus. The purpose of this step is to help you restore your focus.

Clean your workspace, move to a remote location, close your door, and turn off your cell phone. Do whatever you have to do to eliminate distractions.

We realize you can't isolate yourself all the time, but you'll be amazed at what a difference a few uninterrupted hours a week can make. Your productivity will increase, and your attitude will improve.

Step Eight—*Just Say No.* You're a great business owner. You're an involved community player. You're an active member in your trade organization. You serve on several important committees. You're an outstanding parent with active kids. You always help out in the civic clubs you belong to. (No wonder you're burned out.)

A great friend of ours lost his highly successful business solely because he couldn't say no to worthwhile organizations that requested his help. We've worked with scores of small-business owners who were struggling to keep up with their extracurricular activities.

Some entrepreneurs nearly reach a point of personal collapse before they learn to say no. They have since learned to walk away. When they are asked today, they say, "That's a worthy cause, but it doesn't fit my schedule. Thanks for asking, I'm flattered that you would think of me." Stay focused on your highest priorities, and just say no.

Step Nine—*Don't Wade into Sinkholes.* When you are working against a tight deadline on an important project, you may benefit from delaying taking unimportant phone calls, answering e-mail, or going to the Post Office for your mail. Even important activities can become sinkholes when they are not your highest priority.

Checking your e-mail is a classic sinkhole. Accepting unimportant phone calls when you're working against a short deadline is another. Computer games like solitaire are not only sinkholes, they are addictive. (We know an executive who lost his job because his love for the game of solitaire became more important than his work.)

Unnecessary meetings, running errands yourself, and reading the entire newspaper every morning at work are all-time sinkholes. Don't let yourself wander from task to task. Stay on task, and keep your focus. When you need a break, follow the suggestions in Step Ten.

Step Ten—*Find a Diversion.* At times, you'll lose your ability to concentrate on what needs to be done. It happens to everyone, and a good case of burnout makes it worse.

When this occurs, you need a diversion. You need to find a temporary activity that requires a completely different set of skills. For example, if you become bogged down while filling out your monthly inventory forms, take a break and clean some windows, wash the delivery truck, or sweep the warehouse. Limit the diversion to fifteen minutes or half an hour, then go back and finish what you were working on.

Lee Sherman of Hahn Appliance in Tulsa, Oklahoma, finds his diversion in being involved in his community. "I work with community business associations to keep my blade sharp," Sherman admits. "It's good for me, good for burnout, and good for business."

For Jim Chick of Chick's Sporting Goods in Southern California, it's setting aside time for activities he enjoys. "Make sure you set aside personal time for golf, the gym, family, and just relaxing," Chick recommends.

Step Eleven—*Get Some Outside Help.* Business ownership can be one of the truly lonely professions. Business owners often tell us that they talk to people all day long—customers, employees, friends, and so on—but they don't really have anyone to "spill their guts to." If you sometimes feel like the "Maytag man," you may want to seek help outside of your business.

Everybody needs someone to talk to; someone with whom they can share feelings, thoughts, business ideas, and so on. We have found the following resources helpful. Perhaps one of them will work for you. Our suggestions for free help would include: qualified members of the clergy, business mentors, other business owners in your trade association, small-business development center counselors, and some service organizations.

In extreme cases of burnout, you may find it beneficial to hire a professional counselor, psychologist, or psychiatrist to make this step work. The key is to get help. Set your ego and pride aside, and save your health and business.

Step Twelve—*Make Time to Plan.* For many stressed-out business owners, planning can be a time of renewal. Planning can help burnout victims in two ways: 1) it can help them regain their long-term focus on important business elements, and 2) it can help them organize their daily tasks.

Early morning works best for us, but we know others do their most creative planning late at night. By experimenting, you can find the time that is best for you.

Gary Mahn, a partner in Fischer's, a Boise-based copier sales and service company, beats burnout by devoting time to planning new, innovative ideas to make the company grow: "I've found that focusing on new ideas we can use to our competitive advantage helps relieve some of the stress. I also believe in delegating. It's good for management, and gives employees a greater sense of responsibility.

Proverbs 23:7 tells us that the plans of the diligent lead to success. But planning doesn't happen unless we make time for it. We know of no other business activity that generates better long-term, bottom-line results than planning, and it will help you overcome burnout too.

Step Thirteen—*Know When to Quit.* No! We don't mean quit forever. We mean quit for the day or the week. When you reach a point where your efforts are generating more mistakes and frustration than progress, walk away.

If this is happening during the middle of the workday, refer back to Step Ten. If it is happening late in the day, or on the weekends, just stop and walk away.

You don't need to feel guilty about putting some space between you in your work, if you know you gave it your best effort while you were there. We often find that seemingly insurmountable or unsolvable problems become only minor challenges when we tackle them with a renewed mind and a rested body.

Ruth Hanessian, president of the Animal Exchange in Rockville, Maryland, agrees. Ruth said, "After twenty-two years of seven days a week, I'm now closed on Tuesdays. It's important to have some time for yourself."

Step Fourteen—*Redouble Your Efforts.* Sometimes the only way out of a slump is to work your way out. In baseball, we admire great hitters. When the truly great players get into a batting slump, they redouble their efforts. They go in early and take extra batting practice. They spend extra time with the batting coach. They work their way back to excellence.

When we find ourselves in a writing slump, we make ourselves sit down and write. Yes, it takes some discipline, but it works. Here's what we found: Just getting started and putting out a little additional effort will get the motivational juices going again.

Betty Roberts of Focus on Fashion has this observation on effort.

She says, "Work hard while you are at your business, then leave the business at work." A really good idea if you're in a slump.

Step Fifteen—*Love It or Leave It.* Debbie Kramer, owner of Kari Lynn's Formal and Bridal Boutique in McPherson, Kansas, and Berlin G. Myers, Jr., owner of Berlin G. Myers Lumber Corp. in Somerville, South Carolina, both shared this view when asked about beating burnout.

Kramer said, "Love what you do—or move on!" Myers said, "Love what you do; if you don't love it, leave it." Only you can know if you've lost your love for your business. If it's gone, consider moving on.

We believe that most burnout problems are reversible. However, some business situations are not. Many business owners find themselves in a position where they would get out if they could. As a last resort to overcoming burnout, have an exit strategy.

When you've utilized the previous steps and nothing helps, you have two options: 1) Sell the business as a working entity, or 2) Liquidate the assets. Generally speaking, selling the business as a working entity is preferable to liquidating the assets.

We believe that every business owner should have an exit strategy in place early on. Sometimes just knowing that there is a way out will help you refocus and get back on track. When it doesn't, you have a plan B.

A Final Word

As a closing thought, we would like to share a little poem that we've used over the years. We've seen a number of different versions of the poem, but do not know its author.

We believe that it sums up not only how to beat burnout, but how to be that competitor who can take on any business challenge and succeed. We share it with you with the hope that it will inspire you as much as it has inspired thousands of others.

If you think you're beaten, you are,
if you think you dare not, you don't.
If you'd like to win, but think you can't,
it's almost certain you won't.
If you think you'll lose, you're lost,
for out in the world we find,
success begins with a person's will,
it's all in the state of mind.
—Author unknown

Key Points Checklist

☑ Burnout is a common byproduct of hard work and high stress.

☑ Even the most successful business owners have periods of time when it seems that they are walking under their own personal cloud.

☑ Utilizing the right steps and with help, you can overcome burnout and regain your enthusiasm for your business.

Index